The Scaffolding of Spirit

The Scaffolding of Spirit

Reflections on the Gospel of St John

ALAN ECCLESTONE

Darton, Longman and Todd
London

First published in 1987 by
Darton, Longman and Todd Ltd
89 Lillie Road, London SW6 1UD

© Alan Ecclestone 1987

ISBN 0 232 51753 3

British Library Cataloguing in Publication Data

Ecclestone, Alan
  The scaffolding of spirit : reflections on
  the Gospel of St John.
  1. Bible. N.T. John—Commentaries
  I. Title
  226'.507   BS2615.3

  ISBN 0–232–51753–3

Phototypeset by
Input Typesetting Ltd
London SW19 8DR
Printed and bound in Great Britain by
Anchor Brendon Ltd
Tiptree, Essex

Contents

Introduction

> We are beginning to see
> now it is matter is the scaffolding
> of spirit; that the poem emerges
> from morphemes and phonemes: that
> as form in sculpture is the prisoner
> of the hard rock, so in everyday life
> it is the plain facts and natural happenings
> that conceal God and reveal him to us
> little by little under the mind's tooling.
>
> R. S. Thomas, 'Emerging'[1]

The thing that keeps coming back to me is, what is christianity, and indeed what is Christ for us today? The time when men could be told everything by means of words, whether theological or simply pious, is over, and so is the time of inwardness and conscience, which is to say the time of religion as such. We are proceeding towards a time of no religion at all: men as they are now simply cannot be religious any more. Even those who honestly describe themselves as 'religious' do not in the least act up to it, and so when they say 'religious' they evidently mean something quite different.

> Dietrich Bonhoeffer, 'Letters to a Friend'[2]

Recent studies have assembled reasons for believing that the root (of the word religion) is neither that of ligare 'to bind' nor legere 'to gather, to study, to read', but a third root lig-, cognate with Greek ἀλεγω and Albanian *log-, meaning 'to pay attention, to give care', and appearing also in the Latin correlative negative (nec-legere) neglegere, 'to neglect'.

> W. Cantwell Smith, *The Meaning and End of Religion*[3]

WHAT THIS BOOK IS ABOUT

One purpose has shaped this book. It is a plea for learning to read the Gospel according to St John with the kind of attention that can best be described as praying it. In doing that, I believe, we come nearest to the mind and intention of its author. In that way we latch on to what he himself did. He wrote that others might join him. I hope to suggest some ways of setting about it. Here I simply remind myself that it calls for selfless attention, unwearying patience, passionate commitment, honesty of purpose, hunger for truth.

Reading in this way is not foreign to Jewish and Christian traditions of prayer. In just such deliberate fashion Torah was studied and Psalms were recited from time immemorial. They will go on being used in that way for generations to come. My plea is for doing that kind of prayer-reading of the Fourth Gospel. It would be like turning it into a Christian Psalter. Such use of it is greatly needed and long overdue.

Think briefly what is intended. 'The goal is spiritual discernment, the enemy debasement of the religious task', the means the resources that this evangelist long ago gave to his readers.

My title illustrates how we may address ourselves to these three things. I have called it *The Scaffolding of Spirit*, borrowing that phrase from the poem 'Emerging' by R. S. Thomas. In it he uses two figures. The first brings to mind something that we may well have seen in some unfinished statues such as Michelangelo left. In them under the artist's tooling the form imprisoned in the rock appears to be emerging. So, says the poet, under the mind's tooling of the words and experiences of daily life some form may be given to things hidden there. In it lies revelation. The roughest, unlikeliest materials may yield glimpses of things divine.

The second figure is that of building. These same events and facts put into words may well be used as scaffolding for the building of 'the house not made with hands', the home and temple of the Holy Spirit. Such scaffolding is needed or we shall not build much above our workaday foundations. In itself it may appear to be quite crude. We may grow weary of it but learn to value it we must. When we do so we shall see how much there is to hand awaiting use. Stanley Spencer, speaking of his great picture of the resurrection, in the chapel at Burghclere, where the crosses of the battlefields are piled high, called them 'a sort of scaffolding'. The risen Christ is taking them from men's hands, himself the Master-Builder. Our business is at all times to make full use of all resources that daily life affords.

I am suggesting that the Fourth Gospel is one such work of art, a poem tooled by one of the supreme poets of the world. The experiences that went to its making were those represented in part to us by the four gospels. Their authors had much in common. They all drew upon a stock of sayings and stories related to Jesus of Nazareth, partly oral, partly written, derived from various sources. They all shared in the great Jewish religious tradition that bonded together God and his people, a tradition long since committed to writing in the scriptures but maintained as a living force by continuous dialogue within the community. Its basic attitudes best represented in the Psalms are those of trust and expectation. The opening verse of Psalm 40, 'I waited patiently for the Lord: and he inclined unto me and heard my calling', sums up centuries of a relationship with God at once personal and corporate. Its note is to be heard in the Fourth Gospel in Jesus' words: 'I knew that thou hearest me always' (11:42). That trust and expectation in its purity makes for the kind of dependence which allows perfect freedom for development. The forward movements of genuine spiritual growth are checked when the trust begins to falter. At such points in the past the prophets had summoned their hearers to begin again in confident relationship with Israel's God. It was into one such crisis of trust that Jesus of Nazareth stepped.

Great expectations can be sadly distorting of people's lives. That Jesus was greeted with such expectations is evident in all four gospels It is equally clear that almost at once men's opinions divided sharply, making some his disciples and others opponents. Some failed to see the significance of his words and works altogether.

But John did see and did find words to tell what he saw. He stands among the great artists of the world as one not only fortunate and blessed in the experience he had, not only eagle-eyed in his powers of discerning truths, but as a master-craftsman who found words and forms to express and share that vision with others. He was both seer and builder. He saw emerging from the words and works of Jesus the lineaments of a new life for human beings. He sensed in it something whose creative stature was comparable with primal creation. He sought not only to give formal expression to it to guide and sustain his fellow-disciples but to prevent the vision itself being reduced in any way to conform to popular expectations. For that reason, as I shall try to show, he was reluctant to allow titles like Messiah or King of Israel or Son of God to be too easily bandied about. It was because his Christ was so much more than anything that most people understood by these words that he diverted attention from them as much as possible. 'In him was life', such a life as the world had not so far conceived of, a life immeasurably greater than even prophetic expectations, that by all possible means it must be allowed to speak for itself.

This raises a problem of longstanding about John's gospel. Whether he knew the Synoptic gospels or not, he took a markedly different line in presenting his own. So different was it that from early days until now some people have found it difficult to accept. Its historical layout, its unusual sign stories, its language attributed to Jesus, its omissions of many features dear to devotional reflection, have all proved disconcerting. On the other hand many readers approach it through a kind of grid that conflates the four canonical gospels. All of us are probably more accustomed to doing this than we are aware of. Our mental picture of Jesus is most likely to be a composite figure, shaped from the imagery that has appealed to us most. Few hearers of the passages read to them in church services, save students and scholars, are concerned to

4

identify the evangelist who wrote them. If questioned they may well reply, 'Does it matter?' Some will certainly answer that because it is God's word the particular human instrument conveying it to us is not important.

Though I may not convince the latter I shall say that I believe it matters greatly. The singularity of creatures in nature and in human beings in particular is important. We hallow God's name by observing this fact about them. It represents the growing tip of the life that is His and in which we share. It is rightly observed, however briefly, by bestowing a name on each child. The proof that it matters comes uppermost when we learn to love someone, loving them for being that person and no other. The test of the truth of such loving lies in actually discerning that person as she or he is rather than fastening upon them the image we should like them to have. The genuine encounter of persons in loving and being loved turns on knowing their unique and marvellous if often exasperating selves.

I believe furthermore that John the evangelist understood this. He was of course like the others dependent upon common sources of information. Every artist works in that condition. No major work of art is produced in isolation. The greatness of a man's work lies in what he makes of what he receives, in the transmutation of it into a new and singular glory. When John writes, 'and we saw his glory' (1:14), he is introducing his readers to the singularity of his entire gospel. It is no accident that his is the gospel that turns wholly upon the experience of loving, to which we must come later. I would claim it to be the most personal of all the gospels in the sense that is expressed in that phrase concerning 'that disciple whom Jesus loved'. I do not suppose that he did not believe that the love of Jesus did not extend to others. He was ready to emphasise the point that 'Jesus loved Martha, and her sister, and Lazarus' (11:5). But he did face and take fully the overwhelming fact that he was loved. His poem could well carry the title that D. H. Lawrence would use, 'Song of a man that is loved'. No one, I venture to think, would say that this does not matter. It does not make the loved one a perfect artist or husband or friend but it does make the best of that person with all his or her gifts and failings. I do not think John cared much for those great theological systems that men devise to account for and proclaim the ways of God to man. He was no mean theologian but his gospel is not a theological treatise. It is much more a sustained reflection upon the realisation that he was among those whom Jesus loved.

What that did for him this book will try to explore and understand. It made him, I think, more sensitive to personal relationships as the true language of the Spirit. It held him quite firmly to 'that dread point of intercourse', as Browning calls it, with the holy, sparing as he is with the use of that word. It led him to dwell longer than other evangelists on certain key issues in the life of the Christian communities. I am claiming that he was both more mature and far-seeing than other New Testament writers, not infallible but more sure-footed than they, and a better guide in times of crisis like our own.

For that reason there is a special fascination in observing his way of handling material garnered and quarried from the common stock of Jewish and incipient Christian tradition. To a greater extent than others he felt free to choose and arrange it as a great artist does. If that ran the risk of being sometimes dismissed as 'simply fiction', or treated with suspicion as heretical, John took it in much the same way, to cite a modern case, that Ibsen handled nineteenth-century drama. He was convinced that the Spirit-powered church could deal with its problems and hold together no matter what storms internal or external it had to endure. Without fear it could face whatever contemporary circumstances brought to bear upon it.

To do so it would have to be freed from the worldly assumptions about power, authority, glory and dignity which threatened to infect and corrupt human relationships. John came to see that in Jesus these things were not simply magnified to greater dimensions but as often as not completely reversed. It was a difficult lesson to learn and still is. A power that appeared powerless or a glory that looked menial was hard to understand. That John did see what this meant is shown in one of the most dramatic scenes in his gospel.

It concerns the matter of glory, which innumerable Jewish scholars have reflected upon all down the ages. Glory is rightly understood as a manifestation of God, the Shekinah being but one example of it as something almost too dazzling for human eyes to contemplate. The glory of the incarnate Word, of the only begotten Son of the Father (1:14) is asserted in the great prologue to John's gospel. The greatest dignity that could be ascribed to human beings would be to say that they had seen it.

Consider now how John deals with it. It is to be noted first of all that he gives no place to the story of the transfiguration so vividly central to the Markan gospel, though along with Peter and James a John is said to have witnessed it (Mark 9:2–8). He could hardly have deemed it unimportant. At some stage in his gospel he would have wanted to describe how he in company with others saw that glory. He did it in a quite disturbing way. Had he been asked, 'When did you see that glory?' he would have answered, 'When I saw the Lord down on his knees at our feet beginning to wash them' (13:4–12). It was one of the most important things he ever saw. He is one of the truest witnesses to Jesus Christ because he saw the significance of it. The story of the transfiguration is a deeply moving thing but John's feet-washing story turns its notion of glory upside down. John remembered the cry of Peter attempting to stay Jesus from washing his feet as the voice of a man who finds himself being swept from the customary moorings of his life, who knows that he must yield or go away. He noticed that with characteristic abandon Peter yielded and stayed, but one other disciple perhaps at that moment made up his mind that he must go. 'As soon as Judas had taken the piece of bread he went out' (13:30).

The true light and darkness confronting each other could hardly have been more strikingly displayed. John observed it and wrote of it in the words he ascribes to Jesus: 'Now has the Son of Man been glorified, and in him God has been glorified' (13:31). Here is the true pattern of Christian relationships for all time to come. In learning to pray this gospel it may be the best place to begin. 'No servant is greater than his master, no messenger greater than the one who sent him' (13:16). John did not need to add the Matthean words: 'It is enough for the disciple that he be as his master, and the servant as his lord.' His story had made its point. It may, under God, be for us the thing that helps us to stay.

But now we must look at the gospel from a wider angle. In this one incident we have a picture of a few moments in the process of change. The two aspects of such change, conversion and revelation, seeing something and responding to it, are brilliantly portrayed. What it did for John, Peter and Judas we can follow. Men go their different ways when such moments come to them. The gospel however, though constructed out of a series of such incidents, was written from within and addressed to a body of people Perhaps they were grouped in a number of loosely linked communities. Along with their personal experiences of discipleship and in addition to them there was that of belonging to such a movement. It cannot be called a church as yet but it is the church in the making. We must look at it in more detail later. The immediate problems of such a movement were those of self-understanding and their relations with Jewish life as a whole and the pagan world beyond. How were they to find their way?

Scholarly controversy still surrounds the dating of the Fourth Gospel, so that the point at which this evangelist offered his help in the matter cannot be precisely stated. What can be noticed is that, whether written early or late, its way of dealing with the problems is markedly different from that which we find in the Epistle to the Hebrews, the Epistles of Peter, or even of the Pauline Epistles. These latter appear to be more specific about the ways in which the church through its members must deal with such matters of conduct and belief. The Fourth Gospel by contrast offers words of Jesus to be prayed over and a number of images to be reflected upon.

Perhaps the most prominent of such images is that of birth.

It was of course frequently used in the Jewish scriptures. It is an event of almost universal religious provenance. It is used freely in the description of religious experience today, and often much too glibly. At one point in the Johannine record of Jesus' teaching (16:21) it is chosen to give reassurance to the disciples facing their future work. More important still it is introduced early in the gospel (3:1–21) in the conversation with Nicodemus, and is one of the passages most in need of being reflected upon Psalter-wise. Birth is often difficult and dangerous, rebirth not likely to be easier, however we understand it. No timetable can be arranged for the labour pains of a group of people engaged in the process. For the hours of childbirth we must read years in the case of a new community. The suffering that this entails, the fears of those involved in it, the longing for peace and assurance that all is well, all have their full part.

The Fourth Gospel is a book addressed to a community in process of being born. Whether its members see themselves in the matter as the mother – 'the gasping new-delivered mother' – or as the child newborn and crying for comfort and feeding, they are given chapter by chapter what Jesus had said and done to prepare them for it and what they must look for the Spirit to do for them now. But in modern terms this gospel is a manual of obstetrics and post-natal care for the Christian communities. It is the wisest one ever written.

All four canonical gospels treat the appearance of John the Baptist and his summons to repentance as the beginning of the story. They agree that Jesus himself came to be baptised by John. The new movement is to be seen as part of first-century Jewish history, as one among several party formations at the time. It has never been easy to remember that its writings are half-separatist, half-mainstream Jewish in character. The members of the first Christian communities were Jews who had no idea of breaking away from the life of Israel to found a new religion, though their adherence to Jesus gave them a new sense of calling and direction and a new character. At some points they were distinctively committed to a way of life that distinguished them from

Essenes, Zealots or Pharisees of certain traditions. They were drawn and held together by Jesus, spellbound though often baffled by his words. There is both pathos and realism in the phrase attributed to Thomas: 'Lord, we do not know where you are going, so how can we know the way?' (14:5). In later years it was bound to become 'we don't know where we are going either, but we trust you through the Holy Spirit to show us the way'. This is the *raison d'être* of the Fourth Gospel.

My concern is to try to follow and understand how the evangelist sought to present it. It has for me this double importance: in the first place as the ripest spiritual experience of one who lived through those formative years of the Christian community; in the second place as the writing most relevant to the needs of Christian churches in the world today. The birth process of Christ's church is still going on. We as persons and as members of churches old and new are cells in its body being functionally adapted for its continuing life.

What matters most for us is that we get the message of what that really requires of us, so that we cease hanging on to things outdated, overcome our fears of the demands of the future, and listen as sensitively as possible to what the Spirit is saying to the churches today. Those vigorous words addressed to Sardis, Ephesus and the other churches of Asia in the Book of the Revelation may not be the work of the fourth evangelist but they are Johannine in character and intention. They are an urgent reminder to the churches that their business is to give substance to the hope of the world's salvation expressed and shown to us in the person of Jesus Christ. They should send us back to the gospel itself to see what John provided as helps to setting about it. The emergent church of the first century has a great deal to contribute to the emergent church today, as Johannes-Baptist Metz has reminded us,[4] but we shall not learn from it simply by looking backward. All that we learn of the birth process has to be carried forward to meet 'Creation's newest day'.

'That day' (16:26) is a characteristic Fourth Gospel expression. The human calendar does not contain it any more than the political maps of the world give a place to the kingdom of God. The Christian faith nevertheless affirms that the truth of human life lies in the entrance of 'that day' into all our days and of that kingdom into all areas of human experience. In this lay the truly revolutionary nature of Jesus' work. Expectation of both these things was deeply ingrained in Jewish spirituality and to a considerable extent focused in popular imagination upon 'he who would come' to announce fulfilment. What Jesus of Nazareth did, and what I believe John grasped more firmly than most men of that time, was to draw a few men and women round himself to begin living the life of the kingdom whose day had come. The unexpected so far transcended the expectations that the incredulity and hostility that is evident in John's narrative is itself a testimony to the leap of faith that it called for. Nor did it stop there. What John further envisaged and wrote into his gospel was the conviction that the job of the Christian communities lay not so much in preaching about Jesus but in furthering the new way of living sustained by the Spirit that he had bestowed on them.

I repeat then that learning to pray this gospel means becoming familiar with it as the language of the heart as generations of people have done with the Psalms, but using it as the poet suggests as scaffolding to help build the house of the Spirit in our world today. That means that we face the contemporary world scene in terms of religion. A great many events of the past seventy years have compelled men and women of all faiths and denominations to do this. The world wars and the use of nuclear weapons, the holocaust, the changes in sexual behaviour, the ecological problem, the revolution in the technology of communication, and the calling of the Second Vatican Council are all of major import-ance here. Taken together they press on the whole of mankind the question of what is meant by religion as such.

It was posed in personal terms most searchingly by Dietrich Bonhoeffer, the German pastor and teacher who was imprisoned and hanged by the Nazis in Flossenburg in April 1945. During the months before his execution he had thought deeply and written letters about the meaning of the Christian faith and the future role and character of the Christian Church. As an epigraph to this introduction I quote one of the outstanding passages of a letter written in 1944. He observed that 'what we call Christianity has always been a pattern – perhaps a true pattern – of religion'.[5] What would happen in human society if this religious premise should be discarded and the a priori datum of religion's God be set aside? Was it not evident that for a considerable time men had been excluding God from the spheres of morals, politics, science, philosophy and even religion? What was the significance in a world of this character of Christ, the church, the practice of prayer and worship?

Forty years later it might be said that the questions do not quite fit our current experience. Our present perplexities are of a different sort. Religion has returned in a big way in many parts of the world. A new militancy is evident in the Islamic world as also in the relations of Sikhs and Hindus. A popular religion with liturgical and theological expressions of great vitality has appeared among Latin Americans. Africa has witnessed the growth of countless numbers of indigenous churches. The white western religious denominations have flamed with Pentecostal fervour. The Moral Majority has acquired a political as well as a religious force. The attraction of Zen Buddhism and other forms of meditative discipline have found universal response. Yet the polarisation of the world's peoples into affluence or destitution, the threat of nuclear suicide, the breakdown in sexual relations and the increasing violence in civil life, continue to put in doubt the claims being fervently made for religion as such. Ours is not a time of no religion at all but one which raises acutely the question of what we mean by it.

The direction of Bonhoeffer's thought and prayer is nevertheless of great relevance to our reading of the Fourth Gospel. For a considerable time in his letters he referred much less frequently to John's gospel than to the Synoptic writers and St Paul. As time went on he moved ever closer to Johannine thinking. The brief credal summary of verses 1:14–15 'and was made man', became the foundation of his writing and

12

praying. It was to Jesus as man, man pure and simple, the man for others, that he pointed to as the starting point of an attempt to live fully in the world. 'As long as I am in the world,' Jesus had said, 'I am the light of the world' (9:5). The disciples of Jesus must therefore seek him there, going where he went, living as he lived, responding as he responded to the needs of men and women and to the love of God.

It was such a way of life that the churches bearing his name had largely ceased to strive to express, losing thereby the light of life. In failing to do so they had grown more and more remote from and even defensive against the most fundamental claims and needs of common life. They opted rather, as Geza Vermes has said, for 'a doctrinal structure erected upon the basis of an arbitrary interpretation of the Gospel sayings'.[6] They had compromised their calling for the sake of acceptance by the powers of the world. The terms of that acceptance were, as Bonhoeffer realised, being redrafted, and

> He who wept for Jerusalem
> Now sees His prophecy extend
> Across the greatest cities of the world,
> A guilty panic reason cannot stem
> Rising to raze them all as He foretold.[7]

Half a century later it is not only cities like Hiroshima and Beirut, or shanty-towns like Soweto and Sharpeville, but the countryside of Viet-Nam, Nicaragua, the Amazonian forest-land and Africa from Chad to Somalia, that bear witness to the fear and greed of the lords of the world.

Against such a backcloth the Fourth Gospel bids its hearers attend to the words of Jesus of Nazareth: 'but be of good cheer, I have overcome the world' (16:33). A century ago in *The Dream of John Ball*, Morris retold the tale of men's hopes that the Spirit at work in the hearts of men and women would bring them at last through hopeful strife and blameless peace to the 'Day of the King's Son of Heaven'.[8] Today 'the thicket of thorns', as another John called the contemporary world, presses ever more painfully upon the bodies and souls of

God's children but turns our attention all over again to him who believed in the way, the truth and the life made known to the people of God through Jesus Christ, through whom the Spirit lit up the way, made known the truth, and embodied the life that humanity yearns for. Start here with the signs and signposts with which the evangelist John mapped out his gospel.

Before we turn to look at it closely one further reflection upon the meaning of religion may be added, to be kept in mind throughout our reading of John's gospel. We have moved already into the first stages of inter-faith dialogue in several directions and towards a greater concern for the springs of a spirituality that may inform the whole life of every man and woman. They both press for a further clarification of the nature of religion. The word itself has through the ages meant many things. It was used to refer to acts of personal and civic piety, to systems of belief and devotional practices expressive of them. It could still mean to some a mode of life withdrawn from that of the secular world, or a concern for divinity as contrasted with engaging in trade, agriculture, military service or the arts.

Our time has witnessed in fact a marked decline in membership of the major longstanding religious denominations accompanied by the growth outside them of a keener, more widespread interest in the nature of spirituality and its place in the total life of mankind. It has shown an impatience with theological propositions and ecclesiastical forms but a much greater interest in personal relationships and the transcendent aspects of personal life. It may perhaps be described as a return to the concept of virtue as being, in Iris Murdoch's words, 'the same in the artist as in the good man in that it is a selfless attention to nature: something which is easy to name but very hard to achieve.'⁹ She goes on to say that a proper criterion of virtue is right action with the steady extension of the area of strict obligation. At first sight this would seem to many to offer no common ground because it left out God altogether. Not so, she replies, by suggesting that God could be the name of 'a single perfect transcendent nonrepresentable and necessarily real object of attention'. That attention in religious terms is prayer which is the most heart-felt and fullest expression of love. It is no bad exercise to refrain from talking about God in order to give more attention in silence to the obligations of loving, a truly Johannine insight.

What I described above as the religious movement of our time means a shift of attention away from a good deal of the historical presentations of the Christian religion to the more personal aspects of faith expressed in the responses of men and women to each other. What had happened in history was nothing less than a loss of that immediacy of God in Christ which was the very core of the Johannine gospel. What was needed now was the discovery of God in human beings, in other words not by looking backwards to the historical Christ or to an imaginative figure compounded by devotional fervour, but to the men and women in whom through the Spirit he has chosen to live.

It is this shift which gives such immediate relevance to the Fourth Gospel today. It was written, I believe, for men and women who were faced in their religious circumstances by conditions resembling our own. Being Jews they did not need convincing about God. What they needed was God not in the wonderful works he had done in the past but God in their midst. That need was being met. It could not have been more straightforwardly stated than by the simple words of Jesus of Nazareth, 'To have seen me is to have seen the Father' (16:9). All else was illustration and suggestion of what this statement could mean. It is unlikely that John came any more quickly to understanding what it meant than other men and women who heard words to that effect, but his gospel may well have been what a work of art is to any artist who wrestles to bring it about, the way in which he discovers its meaning. He may well have smiled to himself as he wrote that tart reply of Pontius Pilate to his critics: 'What I have written, I have written.' It was the evangelist who would cite the Roman to be his witness.

To round off this movement of religious rediscovery that

invites our attention today, I would instance the line of thought represented in the third epigraph to this introduction. It comes from a footnote to Wilfred Cantwell Smith's book, *The Meaning and End of Religion*.[10] It seeks to establish the word's basic meaning. How valid it is in linguistic terms only experts can say, but in the working and practice of religious life it offers something of great importance. It underpins the thinking already referred to in Iris Murdoch's lectures on *The Sovereignty of God*. A religious attitude is that which is careful to pay full attention to people and things in the process of learning to love them. The contrary irreligious one is that which neglects to do this. It was never more tragically expressed than in Lear's anguished words: 'Oh, I have ta'en too little care of this.'

I suggest that we read the Fourth Gospel therefore as the work of a supreme artist as well as a deeply religious man. What came to him of the words and work of Jesus must have come in many strange and often fragmented forms, infinitely precious yet tantalisingly disordered. He made of them one of the world's greatest poems in the vein of the Psalmist's 'delight in the Lord'. He would have welcomed across the ages, I think, what a fellow poet would one day write:

> Belov'd and faithful, teach my soul to wake
> In glades deep-ranked with flowers that gleam and shake,
> And flock your paths with wonder. In your gaze
> Show me the vanquished vigil of my days.
> Mute in that golden silence hung with green,
> Come down from heaven and bring me in your eyes
> Remembrance of all beauty that has been,
> And stillness from the pools of Paradise.[11]

With that in mind we must now turn to consider more carefully the text of the Fourth Gospel.

1

The Book John Wrote

What first were guessed as points, I now knew stars,
And named them in the Gospel I have writ.
Robert Browning, A Death in the Desert (1864)

St John's Gospel cannot be understood by the mind at all. One
feels in it an emotional excitement on the level of ecstasy.
P. D. Ouspensky, A New Model of the Universe (1984)

One such experience, filled with the discovery of whole-natured
life, is a draught of eternity as deep, sometimes, as a finite life-
time can absorb.
Lancelot Whyte, The Next Development in Man (1944)

An excellent book on the English parish church some years
ago advised the visitor to begin by spending time first of all
simply walking round it. He should notice its shape. He
should observe its features as one would do in looking at
someone's face. He should go on to remark different styles of
building and different materials used. His attention might
well be given to evidences of alterations and extensions, roofs
pitched at new angles, window tracery becoming more elab-
orate and buttresses more daring. He might pause to consider
the significance of a spire or the confident proportions of a
tower. He might take notice of its position in relation to the
village or town it had been built to serve.

In so doing he would recognise in most cases a remarkable
achievement in stone, wood and glass, a blending of ways of
building spread over seven or eight hundred years, a continuity that allowed for varieties of expression. It belonged to

and reflected a changing but always an English sense of style. How much all this would tell him about what went on inside is a matter we must think about later.

In this chapter I want to walk round the Fourth Gospel and look at it from the outside. Like the parish church it is the work of men's hands, an expression of human purpose. The outside look confirms at once that though one man's name is attached to it a great many generations of men have had a hand in it. So many of its features are very clearly derived from different sources. It is a Christian book but much in it is the expression of Jewish experience. I have seen one or two old parish churches in which you could find a Roman arch carried away from a long-vanished military site and built into the fabric of a building used to serve the purposes of a quite different kind of people. Looking at the gospel one may notice something very like that Roman arch in the shape of references to the Passover, a very keystone bit of Jewish history. Just why did the architect of the Fourth Gospel make use of it in this Christian book? Other features only become intelligible when we learn from a commentary what it is to which they refer. Why did Jesus, for example, 'on the last day and greatest day of the festival of Tabernacles' invite people to come to him as to a fountain of living water? Presumably the reference would be clear to those who first heard or read the words. The reader centuries later must consult his guide-book to know why the architect/writer brought it in.

Clearly, continuity means a great deal in this matter. The bonding of old and new features is, as I said of the parish church, a remarkable achievement. Written by a Jew for readers who in the first instance were mostly Jewish, the book is one which generations of Christians like myself have felt belonged to them. But it was continuity that allowed for very great changes, so great that it makes apparent that it upset many people who cared very deeply about it. In all probability it divided friends and members of a family, making them bitter and violent towards each other. When I notice this I am bound to wonder if I have grown so used to reading it my way that I have overlooked the tensions that were there. Has my use of an architectural image stopped short as a visitor's is prone to do of recognising what a trained builder would have in mind, the strains and stresses always at work within the building? I may do well to recall Henry Adams' remark about the great Gothic cathedrals of the Ile de France, that the delight of their aspiration is flung up to the sky, the pathos of their self-distrust and anguish of doubt is buried deep in the earth.[1] No work of art produced in a time of upheaval and change goes quite unscarred by divisive passions even though it may hold them in check.

Walking round them and simply observing may be very perplexing, raising almost too many questions. Few of them seem to have found satisfactory answers. Who was the author of this gospel? For whom, when and where did he write? What purposes had he in mind? Had he read the writings of Paul and the other three canonical gospels? Were his personal intellectual ties with Palestinian or Hellenistic Judaism? Was he worried by and deliberately challenging views and tendencies developing within the Christian communities of his day? Was his gospel an attempt to set the record straight? Is it what most Christians in the modern world need out of all New Testament writings? How best to set about reading it to extract its most valuable food for today?

I turn from these for a moment to ask what seems a much simpler question, what is a gospel? There are but four of them in the New Testament. They therefore belong to a very limited genre. There do exist others that are called Apocryphal Gospels. These are mostly second- or third-century writings existing in fragments or longer forms or in quotations by other writers. They bear important names like those of James, Philip, Peter and Thomas, a literary device, rather than an authentic ascription. One such book known as the Gospel according to the Hebrews and much quoted by early Christian teachers is thought by scholars to have been a divergent form of our Gospel according to St Matthew. Such books were widely in use and much respected. By the end of the second century however the process of including them in or

19

rejecting them from the New Testament canon which had gone on gradually over a considerable time had begun to be decisive. Our four gospels now stood out securely. Irenaeus was ready to argue that 'there could be no more and no fewer than four'. The rest as far as they survive today are of interest as illustrations of how embellished with flights of fancy the basic story of Jesus reached communities of believers scattered all over that area we now call the Near Eastern world. They also remind us that what emerged eventually as orthodox Christian teaching had for lengthy periods to compete with rival interpretations. Christian discipleship began in a world where human enthusiasm and credulity went vigorously to work on the materials out of which the four gospels themselves were first constructed.

It is clearly important to know what any piece of writing is intended to be if we want to follow its meaning. One distinguished critic has argued that unless, for example, we know that a given literary work was intended as a serious tragedy and not a parody, our interpretation of it may go very wrong indeed. He has also insisted that it is too facile to take the view that any work of art means simply what it means to us.[2] In even a very short passage of time the artist's intention may have been forgotten and a quite new significance come to be attached to his work. With the epic or tragedy, the sonnet or the novel, we have hundreds of examples to guide us. The gospels are a rare species and though comparison of one with another helps to give us some sense of common purpose inspiring their writers, their differences have also to be taken very seriously when we discuss their meaning. Too few in number to have moved a critic to do for them what Aristotle did for Tragedy in his *Poetics*, they exhibit enough common features to give us a foothold for attempting to interpret their purposeful character.

They may first be described with a word not altogether in good odour although its strict ecclesiastical use was honest. They were propaganda, an attempt to disseminate or nourish belief in and concerning Jesus of Nazareth. Thus St Mark's work opened with announcing 'the beginning of the Good

News about Jesus Christ, the Son of God'. St Luke described his intention more carefully as being to present an ordered account of the events which led men to embrace certain teachings about them. He now rehearses them to confirm the authenticity of that teaching. They are not designed to convert the outsider but to strengthen the conviction and make more fruitful the lives of believers. St John leaves his purpose in writing unstated until the end of his book. He then speaks of it as 'that you may believe that Jesus is the Christ, the Son of God, and that believing this you may have life through his name'. The gospels quite simply are books about Jesus Christ.

It has been said that Jesus had the good fortune to be written about by five imaginative geniuses. Four of these wrote our canonical gospels. The fifth writer was St Paul who started from a quite different point and cast all his work in a different mould. The evangelists aimed at telling a story to exercise and thus strengthen the believers' part in it. They say in effect this is our story too because we are in Jesus Christ and he is in us. But to say this about them is to go inside the building, which I want to defer a little longer to appreciate the better what unusual writings they are. They are not without features which relate them to a much more extensive literature.

This can best be described by comparing them with a single play in a trilogy such as Aeschylus or Sophocles wrote for Greek theatre, but allowing for one big difference. The Greek audience knew the whole story in general terms. In the literature of which the gospels are the second play of the trilogy, the first part had been written up long since in the Jewish scriptures. The third has yet to be known and remains unwritten because the end is not yet, but the writing is still in progress. The second very clearly continued the story begun in the first but gave it so unexpected a denouement that many were quite baffled and turned away from it while others rejoiced. 'They looked as they had heard of a world ransomed, or one destroyed: a notable passage of wonder appeared in them; but the wisest beholder, that knew no more

but seeing, could not say if th'importance were joy or sorrow.'[3]
You had to be truly inside the story to read its meaning aright
but it needed a lot of rehearsing.

It is now some years since Dr Aileen Guilding set out in
great detail the thesis that the Fourth Gospel was written
with a view to providing lections for use in the synagogues of
Christian Jews, the movement that had grown out of the work
of Jesus, arranged in a three-year cycle and giving special
attention to the well-known Jewish festivals. I believe that it
deserved more consideration than it received then or since.
It is true that we have too little exact information about
synagogue practice at the time to give firm foundation to it.
The textual coincidences relating John's work to the Old
Testament readings appear in some cases to be almost too
apt. On the other hand the Fourth Gospel gives great prominence to those festivals. It mentions three Passovers, the feast
of the Dedication and that of Tabernacles, and another
referred to simply as a Jewish festival (5:1). It associates Jesus
very closely with their observance and uses each occasion to
allow him to expound his distinctive teaching. Whether or
not Christians actually used the Fourth Gospel in the way
suggested, the writer's intention of bonding traditional
observance with new significance appears to be solidly lodged
in the text.

Be that as it may the gospels began with an emphasis upon
continuity with that first great drama of Israel's calling and
expectation of the One who was yet to come. Our outside
view of them takes notice of all the historical and social
references, including those specifically religious which the
various writers used to make this clear. Matthew's determi-
nation to make the bonding with the whole biblical story
led him to begin with a genealogy of Jesus beginning from
Abraham, and subsequently to lose no opportunity to point
out fulfilment of prophetic insights about the one who was to
come. Mark had most probably set the line to be followed by
relating the prophecy of Isaiah to the coming of John the
Baptist whose appearance signified the raising of the curtain
upon the new play. Luke was to take a further step to empha-

sise the historical setting within the Roman and Jewish worlds. John was to prove even bolder. His beginning, like that of the first play, gave a universal significance to what was now to take place by relating it to the Genesis story.

At this point, if I may return to the architectural view, the masonry shows some signs of agitation. Did the John the Baptist campaign fit so neatly into the story of Jesus as the gospels seem to want to suggest? All testify to the Baptist's acknowledgement of the unique status of Jesus, his discernment of the hour and the man fulfilling all expectations. The most obvious next step would surely have been to throw himself publicly behind Jesus and to lead his disciples en masse in that direction. But there is no evidence that he did so. According to Mark Jesus waited until the arrest of the Baptist by Herod before starting to proclaim the good news of the Kingdom. Luke tells us that while lying in prison the Baptist sent some of his disciples to ask Jesus himself whether he was really the one they had looked for.

Now one cannot build or use scaffolding rightly with such uncertainty in mind. John therefore went very deliberately to work on the matter. He first of all inserted into the original text of his prologue hymn certain verses emphatically denying that the Baptist was the light and insisting that he was simply a witness to it. It suggests that there was a need to do this. Though some of the first followers of Jesus had been among those attending on John the Baptist, it becomes clear (2:23–30) that John himself went on baptising with his own following disciples about him. The evangelist meant to settle the problem by reporting that the Baptist had told them somewhat graphically that 'he must grow greater, I must grow smaller', after which no more is said about him. To revert to the dramatic presentation of the story, it looks as if the Baptist's followers would not leave the stage and were still in action years later when John was writing his gospel.

Having turned that awkward corner John set to work upon the whole structure he had in mind. His prologue consisted of a tenon and mortice jointing of two planes, verses 1–18 in which the great cosmic action takes place, and verses 19–51 in which the action on earth and in history is set in motion. The first players in the human caste are recruited. The first intimations are given that the sound waves have excited both Galileans and Jews to expect something dramatic.

It happens at once. Jesus cleanses the temple. Before we consider John's intention in starting with this, it is important to look at the whole block that now comes into view (chs 2–12). It consists of a series of signs or significant stories interspersed with lengthy statements by Jesus expounding his teaching about his own work delivered to increasingly hostile crowds. It is to be noted that John departs from the Synoptic tradition by taking Jesus backwards and forwards from Jerusalem to Galilee many times. From the outset this is no outburst of Galilean turbulence but a matter affecting and springing out of Israel's entire history. Whether John knew or did not know words which Luke attributed to Jesus about going up to Jerusalem – 'it would not be right for a prophet to die outside Jerusalem' (Luke 13:33) – it is clear that he meant to put all the emphasis he could upon the prophetic aspect of Jesus' words. He is the one who lays bare the truth of this moment in history and of the various roles that people are playing in it. Some healings are included among the signs but John was not concerned to give prominence to healing lepers or casting out evil spirits, the miracles or mighty works which attracted such attention to themselves rather than to their significance in the whole drama. John's intention may be compared with the way in our own day Thomas Kuhn has written about making revolutions in modes of thinking, when some men begin to discard the paradigms that have hitherto sustained their thought and turn to new ones. He had grasped the point that with the coming of the Logos-Christ into human history nothing could remain unaffected. He therefore set out to show in the series of signs what had now to be faced.

There is something almost breathless in the unfolding of this. Religion freed from huckstering; sexual relations must find a way of giving women their rightful place, paternalism must be set aside, sectarian and tribalist divisions must cease,

24

MAY·HE
SUPPORT·US
ALL·THE·DAY
LONG,·TILL·THE·SHADES
LENGTHEN·&·THE·EVENING
COMES,·AND·THE·BUSY
WORLD·IS·HUSHED·&·THE
FEVER·OF·LIFE·IS·OVER·&
OUR·WORK·IS·DONE
THEN·IN·HIS·MERCY·:·:·
MAY·HE·GIVE·US·A·SAFE
LODGING·&·A·HOLY·REST
AND·PEACE·AT·THE·LAST.

CARDINAL·NEWMAN

agonising about the temple must give way to recognition of a profounder spirituality, the dispossessed of society must not be thrust back into making futile rebellions, the needy must be treated as of right and mortality must not be allowed to be the great fearful negation of life. In very truth a greater than Moses is here yet the situation is one that Moses himself foretold. Human history was not intended to culminate in the Exodus and the covenant. These were but Act One. Now Act Two had begun and the spiritually awake must take up their parts.

Clearly the praying of all these chapters is a matter of seeing their relevance at any time to the human condition. The Synoptists recall the many warnings given by Jesus about being awake to the coming of the kingdom, and though John does not use such words he conveys the same sense of urgency. Unless men feel the wind of the Spirit they will be dead to the summons that calls them to the new life. The prayer that the reader must make is that of the Psalmist: 'Lighten mine eyes, that I sleep not in death'. It is in that context that we must read and pray the last of the great sign stories of which the key-word is: 'I am the resurrection'. The gist of the warning is in explicit terms: 'You who are so familiar with the great drama of Israel's past, take care that you do not fail to perceive the new play that is being enacted under your very eyes! Ask yourselves whether your familiarity with it has not lost its essential spirit.' If the question were put why, with all their knowledge of the scriptures, so many refused to listen to Jesus, he himself, according to John, supplied the answer: 'You have not the love of God in you' (5:42).

With Chapter 13 we come to that part of the building which can best be likened to the sanctuary of our parish church. Of all the four gospels this gives us the most sustained and intimate account of Jesus speaking with his disciples. Here our outside view can tell us little save for the feet-washing scene which I have called John's version of the trans-figuration, so that that little prayed over scene may, seen from inside, 'become my universe that sees and knows'. On the other hand the silence of John concerning the traditional

institution of the Eucharist, comparable with but more startling than his omission of the story of the actual baptism of
Jesus, compels attention. It has long been recognised that
there are signs of misplacement in the text of these chapters
which culminate in the great final prayer of Jesus for his
disciples. The most obvious is the ending of Chapter 14 with
the words, 'Come now, let us go,' followed by three more
chapters continuing the scene in the supper room. The
absence of anything that overtly could connect the meal itself
with the Passover has also given rise to lengthy discussion.

Immense ingenuity coupled with erudition of generations
of scholars has not produced explanations of John's departure
from the tradition of the Passover meal represented in the
Synoptic accounts convincing enough to carry general
approval. Viewed from the outside it must remain inexplicable. Only when we are ourselves reading it from within does
the full weight of John's overall purpose become apparent.

Abrupt contrast of darkness and light, confusion and calm-
ness, falsehood and integrity marks the next two chapters.
Brute force represented by a detachment of the temple guards
and a cohort of Roman soldiers now supplies the initiative in
the action. The emphasis on love in the preceding chapters
is matched by that on power. The polarity of human relationships is indicated as starkly as possible. John says nothing of
the agony in the garden which in the Synoptic accounts figure
as among the most revealing expression of Jesus' humanity.
He likewise omits that most telling phrase of Matthew's
account, the words spoken by Jesus to Judas: 'Friend, where-
fore art thou come?' Keeping fixedly to objective reporting
John details the steps by which the theme of the renunciation
of power implicit in the very presence of Jesus in the world
is upheld to the end. John had at a much earlier stage of his
writing insisted that Jesus had accepted the taking of his life
by the worldly powers as an unquestionable part of the task
he had taken on, indeed was sent to do. There are traces in
all the gospels that the disciples were not entirely convinced
of this and, as in Matthew and Luke together with John, were
ready to make a fight of it. An Islamic writer has said that

Christians must needs be sad men because the disciples did not venture their lives to deliver their master.[4] John's gospel made it clear none the less that that kind of power struggle had been wholly set aside by Jesus himself. He did not surrender his life that his friends might escape but that they might learn to live in his spirit and not that of the world.

John's passion story is hewn from the hardest imaginable rock. It is meant to bear the heaviest of burdens, a faithful contention with death. It brings into view the institutions of human polity, religious, military and judicial. In the midst of them it sets a prisoner. It confronts every reader with the common but terrible situation in which men can do to another man what they will. It is the moment when the Satan of this world lifts his head and laughs, when the victims must wonder if a different world could exist or whether the idea that the world that we have can be loved is not dreadful mockery after all. Notice that but for the description of 'that disciple whom Jesus loved' repeated once more there is no further reference to love in this gospel except in the added twenty-first chapter.

We must try to look steadily at this part of the fabric of John's gospel. It is probable that all of us are tempted to turn away from it and to seek comfort and meaning in some theological statement or symbolic artefact like a crucifix which no longer makes us shudder. We do not face the problem of God's presence in human history unless we bring all human history into perspective. I go back at this point to the question of paying attention, of actually seeing our fellow man. Simone Weil wrote of the frightful spectacle of the prisoner in the hands of a few men deciding his fate by a word and paying no attention to him.[5] In his novel *L'Etranger*, Albert Camus has pictured much the same scene from another angle. Elie Wiesel writing as a survivor of Auschwitz has said that 'it signifies not only the failure of two thousand years of Christian. civilisation, but also the defeat of the intellect that wants to find a Meaning – with a capital M – in history'.[6] What Auschwitz embodied has none. John Hick concluded that such suffering remained a mystery, impenetrable to the rationalising human mind. Whatever else it was written for,

the Fourth Gospel was not written to supply a happy ending
to human history. Yet John had an end in view. He wrote
with the conviction that Jesus had completed the work he
had been sent to do and that his last word from the cross
meant simply that. Very briefly indeed he wrote into his
account certain resurrection appearances, hinted at Ascension
and concluded with a final reference to the gift of the Holy
Spirit. Our journey round the outside looks somehow incon-
clusive if we expected something more incontrovertibly
proven by all that had taken place. The end, it appears, is
simply a beginning. This man stands once again before the
world like Joseph had been pictured to stand before the
brothers who had tried to get rid of him and to whom he now
said: 'God sent me before you to preserve your lives' (Gen.
45:5), and repeated later, 'you thought to do me evil, but
God meant it unto good, to bring to pass as it is this day, to
save much people alive' (Gen. 50:20). He stands before the
world in the persons of those who believe in him even though
they have not seen anything more than someone dying with
an unswerving trust in God.

No more but so? There have been not a few Christian
readers who have been disconcerted by this. Nathaniel
Micklem spoke for some of them when he wrote: 'I had for
some time been reading (and possibly avoiding) the Fourth
Gospel with the feeling, "this is wonderful, this is beautiful,
this may be spiritually true, but it didn't happen." '[7] Others
may have commented more gently, 'Did it happen like that?'
Taking a look again at the outside of this gospel so many are
disconcerted by the absence of parables that have lodged
themselves in human memory, such as the Good Samaritan
and the Prodigal Son. They miss the Jesus who spoke of the
lilies of the field, the sensitive guest who noticed the slightest
shades of human behaviour, the Jesus of the Lord's Prayer
and the Sermon on the Mount. Instead they are met by one
who speaks so constantly of himself, whose 'I' is frequently
on his lips, who slips away when he wills from the crowds.
'There is,' says Barnabas Lindars, 'a lack of human warmth
in the portrait of Jesus that requires the complement of the

Synoptic picture to convey the truth.'[8] Not a few critics have spoken of being more repelled than attracted by this Jesus. Some have found him a scarcely credible figure, out of contact with his fellow-men.

It is right that we should face these things whether they come from others or arise within ourselves. However they come they are an indication, in the architectural picture I have used in this chapter, of something ill-fitting, not so much now in the fabric but in its relation to the human community it was built to serve. Our gospel, we have said, stands to the world of men and women as an assertion of the reality in their lives, of what von Hügel called the is-ness rather than the ought-ness which is the real meaning of religion. Reading it many centuries after it was written we are bound to ask how it has fared since those first days. What has the changing climate known to us in the sunshine and gales of medieval Christendom, the Renaissance, the Reformation, the Enlightenment, the French Revolution, and industrial, scientific, technological change, done to its position? Is it, as Matthew Arnold wondered, like some fallen runic stone, a thing of the past? In the churchyard of the village in which I live stands one of the most beautiful stone crosses erected to make the kind of assertion I have just mentioned. It dates from more than a century before the Norman Conquest and appears to commemorate the putting away of pagan gods and the acceptance of the gospel of Jesus Christ. What was the reality apprehended by those people who made that momentous change? Yesterday it was represented by Wotan and Thor and Loki, today by the God and Father of Jesus Christ. Is it still so?

It is a question that cannot be answered until we go inside this gospel building. Before we do so however it is important that we decide what it is that we are going to look for. Religion is essentially paying that kind of attention which is adoration. It strives to know that which it adores. Our Fourth Gospel puts it very directly: 'Eternal life is this: to know you, the only true God, and Jesus Christ whom you have sent' (17:3); but its fabric as I have called it puts another question

29

continually to us. How well, how rightly, do we know him?
If at all times our knowledge of him can be but partial and
often distorted, by what steps do we come to the fuller and
purer knowledge, to the light of Truth? It is with that in mind
that we may now go inside.

2

The Poem We Read

Here Love's divines – since all divinity
Is love or wonder – may find all they need.

John Donne, Valediction to his Book

Here words would lead a man to Paradise if he could listen to
what they have to say.

Julien Green, *Diaries* (1941)

He was absolutely determined – as he often pointed out Coleridge
was – to re-instate the Logos as a living power, to demonstrate
in poetry itself the Word made flesh.

K. S. Lynn, F. O. Matthiessen, *Masters*

Our business now is with seeing, with the kind of seeing
which Wordsworth described as one of the great gifts of a
poet. He spoke of it as using an 'inward eye' and of 'seeing
into the life of things'. We go to the poets to have our eyes
opened to see in that way. John the evangelist was a seer and
poet of that kind. He had learned to see into the things
concerning Jesus. He had seen with an inward eye their
significance for the world. He wrote his gospel that others
might share as fully as possible in it. We who read it today
have opportunity to do that.

It could only be done in the first place by using the
language of poetry. We have to learn to read it as such. That
language is a language of symbols as indeed that of religion
must always be. It involves using words not just to indicate
things but to try to convey to others something which lies
beyond such references. In using them in this way the writer

31

is not deceiving himself or his readers. He is trying to communicate or share with them the total experience he has had, the emotions, the thoughts and the attitudes to which it gave rise. Things hidden within it or lying beyond it are brought into view. To bring this about he employs a sign-language. His words point beyond their ordinary use. In reading a poem we have therefore to learn how to follow the signs being used. The artist, David Jones has reminded us, 'deals wholly in signs'.[1] He is not making statements about various things but using fictions to draw us all into an imaginative communion with him.

Such an artist proceeds by way of re-presentation. He recalls certain things in a way that permits us to enter into them now. To do so he makes use of words, imagery, references, feelings and ideas which are already common to the life of his readers. In the gospels that means all the wealth of imagery that had been in constant use throughout Israel's history. It included those directly religious which spoke of God as Father, Judge, Maker and Ruler. It took from nature those of water and wind, fire and storms, bread and wine, light and darkness, birth and death. From Israel's history it drew imagery in such terms as Messiah, Son of God and Son of Man, the Spirit as dove, the temple as God's dwelling place among his people, the Passover and the covenant as the symbols of his relationship with them. Such imagery put to use century after century provided the forms through which this people discerned and responded to the reality of their very existence. We could liken it in visual terms to an enormous tapestry woven from the total experience of generations of men and women but to do so would run the risk of using too static an image. Hebrew symbolism is always expressive of action, of things being done and relationships entered into. For that reason too it swings between singing and keeping silent.

The Fourth Gospel drew freely upon this great treasury of Israel's experience concentrated in the enacted imagery of its festivals and daily practices which kept alive the memories and hopes of the nation. It did so because Jesus himself had used it and John's writing would have been unintelligible without it. What we his readers today have to do, since we no longer stand immediately in that tradition but are heirs of its subsequent Christian restatement, is to learn how to read it aright.

It means three things. First learning what the initial situation in which Jesus figured was like. In the second place understanding what the evangelist saw Jesus doing in it. Thirdly we have to translate what John wrote into terms which are relevant and meaningful today. All such reading of poetry is in a very real sense an act of personal translation. The miracle performed by words is nowhere more vividly shown than in the fact that through an immensely long chain of translations the poem John wrote reaches us today to draw us into the experience it expresses.

What then was the groundwork from which it sprang? We cannot read very far into this gospel without being made aware of figures in a landscape and a certain historical scene. The venue is Palestine in the first century. It is peopled with Jews whether living in Galilee or Jerusalem, and with Samaritans lodged in a countryside between. Towards the end of the narrative we also encounter some Romans holding power in this occupied territory. The poem is no romantic dream or mystical vision but the expression of something that took place in the towns and villages of that countryside. Its roots are in history.

At this point we have to see that this means our reading has to be in a sense bi-focal. We read what John's poem gives us but we also draw upon a much wider reading matter. This is comprised of all that we learn from historical studies of Jewish life at that time and also from the vast literature concerning the religious experience of that people set out in the scriptures. How much his readers knew of that and how much they were influenced in their thinking by it John does not tell us because he took it for granted. Only in a few cases does he make a comment, for example saying that Jews had no dealings with Samaritans, and he saw no reason to stop and tell us why. All our modern reading of the gospels is affected by this. They are not wholly self-explanatory and not always in full agreement with what modern historical and biblical scholarship can tell us. In so far as we have immersed ourselves in those Jewish scriptures we can appreciate the better the climate of opinion that the gospels presupposed but from which they had also to some extent turned away. Breakaway bodies may not always be quite the best witnesses to the state of affairs from which they departed. It is therefore good that Christian readers in the interests of truth should always be ready to hear what Jewish writers have got to say about the gospels.

Because this book comes from a Jewish religious tradition its roots are deep in the literature which was the expression and nurturing force of its experience. A religious assessment of the life-work of Jesus would have lacked its true dimensions had it not grounded itself in the scriptures. John therefore insisted on going back to the very beginning of things as did the writer of Genesis. He set his own poem in that framework of vision. In the story of Jesus the creative power of the Godhead must be seen to be active.

The next step he took was not so clearly indicated in a vivid phrase but was none the less as deliberate. He went on to recall his readers to the experience set out in the Book of Exodus. There were two very good reasons for doing so. First because Exodus is the very foundation of Jewish life. They are the people of the Exodus. Secondly because John saw in the work of Jesus the re-enactment of that event and the nature of the Christian community in relation to it. The ground-base of all the discussions of Jesus with his critics is a reference to the Exodus experience.

What then did it signify to Jewish people? It comprised a number of stages. The first of these was that of liberation, the second the life in the wilderness, the third the acceptance of the covenant, and the fourth the entry into the Promised Land. All were to become paradigmatic to John as he thought of the life of the Christian community for which he was writing. His job was to set out these things as stages of understanding through which all the members of the Chris-

34

tian communities must make their way. They too must set
out on a Long March not in geographical terms with a charis-
matic leader like Moses but no less deliberately breaking
free from the power-structured society, religious and political,
communal and personal, in which they had grown accustomed to live. It was in no sense to be an escape from history
but a sober attempt to go through the birth pangs and travail
of a new kind of community being born. It would involve
persecution and most probably death even though it would
try to live peaceably with all men. It would neither turn its
back on the world nor use worldly methods to overthrow its
opponents. The test of its integrity would lie in its practice.

If John, as is generally believed, wrote late in the first
century he knew a good deal about the second phase of the
Exodus. This was the time when the hardships of going on
steadily with the new venture and facing the tensions
developing inside the communities would be most keenly felt.
There would be those who turned back in their hearts to the
old way of life, making a rosy picture with which to contrast
their present hardships. There would be others who sought
to solve their problems by igenious compromises with the
social order prevailing around them. The real test lay in
whether they would try to think out and put into practice the
new modes of living which their journey to freedom presupposed. How much self-criticism and internal dispute would
they allow and encourage for the sake of the truth in living
that they sought? Could they work with a sense of unity not
imposed from above but inspired from all those participating
in it? As we read the Fourth Gospel do we get from it deep
conviction that the guidance of the Holy Spirit is a matter
for real rejoicing?

The third phase they moved towards was that of renewed
sense of covenanted relationship with God and the taking
upon themselves of the new Law in the name of Jesus. There
is but one commandment that is called new in this gospel,
'That ye love one another as I have loved you.' In the First
Epistle of John it is this which shines out in all the writer is
trying to say. 'It is a new commandment because the night

is over and the true light is now shining.' What the fullness of living in that Spirit will be like is the coming at length to the land of promise. The conviction that they will come to it is nourished throughout the years by the words of Jesus: 'I have overcome the world.'

With this Exodus story in mind as the foundation of all that John wrote we turn now to his presentation of it. In speaking of it as poetry I do not mean that it was written in one of the poetic forms of Hebrew or Aramaic literature of the time. Some scholars have supported that view. That certain passages in the New Testament were composed to be used as hymns seems probable enough. The first eighteen verses of the Fourth Gospel may well have been used in this way. Nor am I thinking of a poet as the writer of verse, the layout of whose work on the page distinguishes it from prose. We need a much wider conception of poetry than that which rests on the technicalities of diction and metrical forms, important as these have been. We can learn much from Herbert Read's contention that the representative poet of the United States of America was not Walt Whitman but the novelist Henry James in virtue of the width and depth of his vision or what he called the 'very range and inclusive splendour of his perceptual apprehensions'. Wallace Stevens saw the dividing line between prose and poetry marked by the poet's attempt to discern an inner reality in human affairs in conflict with and denied by the worldly choices that men and nations could be tempted to make. John saw the conflict in twofold fashion. He tells us at great length and with much detailed observation what it looked like in the working life of Jesus. He prefaced that account with a much shorter perception of what was at stake; that the true light of life had come into the world in Jesus Christ and been rejected by a great many people, but to some he had given his own light and spiritual strength to enable them as children of God to set about their Exodus journey.

John's deliberate return to the Word that was 'in the beginning' made clear what the inner reality of experience in that short period which Jesus spent at work in Galilee and Judaea meant to him. It was nothing less than the primal purity of Creation which he wanted his poetry to convey.

> The poem refreshes life, so that we share
> For a moment, the first idea. It satisfies
> Belief in an immaculate beginning
> And sends us, winged by an unconscious will
> To an immaculate end. We move between these points.[2]

It takes but little imagination to realise that the day to day life of those making the new Exodus journey must have closely paralleled that of their ancestors. The recapitulation of the tedious arguments between Jesus and his critics which makes up so large a part of the first twelve chapters of this gospel served to throw into greater relief the boldness with which John set forward 'the first idea'. No other great poem began with such breadth of vision. Recall the first lines of *Paradise Lost:*

> Of Man's first disobedience, and the fruit
> Of that forbidden tree whose mortal taste
> Brought death into the world . . .

which provide a chillingly impressive introduction to the great drama that follows and leave readers in no doubt about the solemnity of the issue of human salvation. Yet its significant words, disobedience, forbidden, mortal and death, contrast starkly with the light, life, grace, truth and glory with which John expounded his announcement of the divine Word, the Logos as living power coming into the world of men.

Look briefly at the great epics, at the *Iliad* that tells us that 'it was Apollo that began the feud', at the *Aeneid* which in trumpet tones declares, 'Arms and the man I sing.' In both cases we are in the world of warriors where all day long the noise of battle rolls and 'sad mortality o'ersways their power'.

In English we have but one modern epic, Hardy's *The Dynasts*, to consider. It too provides a diminished perception of what is at stake though it begins in the Overworld among a strange company of spirits:

37

> Shade of the Earth
> What of the Immanent Will and Its designs?
> Spirit of the Years
> It works unconsciously, as heretofore,
> Eternal artistries in Circumstance

and we realise at once that the lines of communication are severed. These phantom intelligencies contemplate the drama on earth but remain worlds apart. Set against this the brief comment that John has Jesus making at the end of his opening chapter: 'You will see heaven open and, above the Son of Man, the angels of God ascending and descending upon him'. Should we turn back to Goethe's *Faust*, the prologue recalling our gospel begins boldly in heaven but narrows down its perspective of earth to a scholar's study and sinister juggling with spirits. Even if we turned to Wordsworth's poetry of the renovating spirit which he felt to be at work in nature, we cannot but be conscious that the literature of the modern world has, with a few exceptional cases, moved away from the basic beliefs of both Jewish and Christian communities. The great assertion that underlies the Fourth Gospel, the divine Word taking human flesh, has for increasing numbers of men and women largely ceased to be meaningful. 'God has become a Deus absconditus, hidden somewhere behind the silence of infinite spaces, and our literary symbols can only make distant allusions to him, or to the natural world which used to be his abiding place and home.' How then can we read the Johannine poem? Is there any place left in the world of today for religious poetry at all? Must it be of significance to believers only? These questions have been pressing for attention for several centuries now. My plea for reading John's gospel as a religious poem must be able to answer them fairly.

In calling it a religious poem I do not wish to put it alongside Wordsworth's *Ecclesiastical Sonnets* or Keble's *Christian Year*. I want rather to keep it in company with the poetry of Dante, Goethe and Blake, no less than with that of Chaucer and Shakespeare, Keats, Arnold and Yeats. Some objections however have still to be faced.

Two centuries ago Dr Johnson while writing his life of Waller, a poet he respected, took exception to his devotional poetry. He argued that the relation of man with his Creator and Judge was not a sphere into which human words should intrude. The Word that became our redeemer should alone speak there. Inventiveness on the part of a writer at such a juncture could not but be quite distasteful. Johnson therefore magisterially pronounced: 'Omnipotence cannot be exalted, Infinity cannot be amplied, Perfection cannot be improved.' The case for religious poetry was dismissed. Fortunately neither patriarchs nor prophets, psalmists nor evangelists had believed this at all. Abraham had argued with God. Isaiah admitting freely that human lips were tainted none the less believed that the Holy One wanted to reason together with men. Job's author desired nothing less than that the Almighty would answer his complaints. The later Isaiah called on those who kindled a fire to walk in its light and sparks. That, as the American critic R. P. Blackmur remarked, was 'a motto for poetry, a judgement of poetry, and a poetic gesture which carries the prophetic meaning of poetry'.[3]

The objections continued. Among them was that of T. S. Eliot who conceded that such poetry might have a minor place in the world's literature but no more because it dealt with too limited a range of human experience. 'It left out', he said, 'what men consider their major passions.'[4] With Dante and Donne in mind we may well catch our breath at this. What truth there was in Eliot's words was largely a criticism of the editors of anthologies of religious verse. In any case he then changed his mind and began to count not only Dante but Corneille and Racine as great religious poets.

The charge of limitation was more forcefully made somewhat later by Dame Helen Gardner in her Ewing Lectures on Religious Poetry. Taking Donne as an example she contrasted his uninhibited love-poetry with that which he wrote on religious matters. 'In the field of religion', she said, 'it is not what I feel but what I ought or ought not to feel'[5]

39

which is being expressed. She went on to describe religion as something given rather than invented, handed down in rituals and rules of conduct obligatory both personally and socially. It followed that a religious man wrote 'in fetters', asking his readers to accept, during the readir,y of his poem at least, truths which were not presented as personal discoveries and values which were not his. His job was to prove or maintain his religious credentials.

Such a view of religion and poetry would undoubtedly debar the evengelist John, the Psalmist, the authors of Job and the Song of Songs among others, from being considered great poets. It would reduce their literary stature to that of Thomas Tusser writing his *Five Hundred Points of Good Husbandry* or Michael Drayton surveying England in his *Poly-Olbion*. It would cut the ground from under the feet of Blake, Coleridge and Arnold. That much religion is of the kind described above must be admitted though I find the idea of something 'given rather than invented' a strange way of describing religious experience. The two things which distinguish the Fourth Gospel's account of it are love and truth, the givenness of which, like the covenant itself, has no force until it be freely accepted either by this or that person or a community. From that moment onwards it must be tested in practice and found to be true, to be real, to be worth living and dying for.

Religion seen in terms of the Exodus is not a matter of things handed down but of confrontation, of coming up to a place where divine revelation and human discovery meet. As thought is born of failure, poetry derives its vital force from the poet's imaginative grasp and expression of what has hitherto eluded him. At that moment of 'kindling', as the Wordsworths called it, he is able to tell of something that alters his whole vision of life. Revelation is never a one-sided affair like filling a vessel. It is always a participation in something between two parties.

Two classic illustrative moments which stand almost equidistant in time on either side of the Fourth Gospel may illustrate this. The first is that of Moses' experience at the

burning bush. The theophany does not begin until he turns
aside to look at it nor is it ever completed until his life ended.
The second is begun at the moment when Dante, not quite
nine years old, saw Beatrice Portinari at a May day party, a
girl younger than himself, and began to know that a god
stronger than himself had touched him, kindling in him inspiration that would bear its fruit many years later in the greatest
poem of medieval Europe. John tells us nothing of any such
moment that began his discipleship though he may have been
one of the two mentioned in the first chapter who stayed with
Jesus. If then he be 'that disciple whom Jesus loved' spoken
of later, the Fourth Gospel is a love story like the *Divina
Commedia* itself.

No writer or artist could have laid greater emphasis upon
seeing. Not only does the word occur many times but one of
the most vividly told sign stories, that of giving sight to the
man born blind, teased out in detail puts the whole problem
of seeing before John's readers. It is noticed as a very grave
problem rooted deep in Israel's history no less than in that
of pagans. Like the other evangelists John quotes Isaiah about
blinded eyes and ununderstanding hearts, and many times
comments sadly upon people's failure to see the glory of what
was being enacted before them. It is not to be supposed that
John excluded himself from the unseeing disciples at many
critical points in his gospel. Many times over it is they who
are said to have been baffled.

> Blessings emblazoned that day;
> Everything glowed with a gleam;
> Yet we were looking away.[6]

The consequences of not seeing were grave. It was not simply
that men missed the many-splendoured thing but that in their
blindness they turned with a fear and ferocity to attack what
they failed to comprehend, and themselves passed judgment
upon their world.

For that reason too John went to all possible lengths to
present Jesus as the opener of men's eyes. He wrote of him
as one who could tell what was in a man or woman, as one

who saw beyond the masks that men make for themselves and the labels that others stick on them. Such insight into others such as is mentioned in speaking of Nathanael has indeed been turned into a charge of unreality attaching to the human nature of Jesus. This is where once again we need the artist to help us to translate fear into love so that in our dealings with one another we discern the true form (morphē) of the other one, and are able to appreciate his or her singular beauty. Our approaches, it has been said, must be those which coax a revealing rather than those that command.

I turn to Frederick Franck's fine book, *The Zen of Seeing*, as the most valuable guide on this matter and one that illuminates all that I here try to say about things seen as the scaffolding of Spirit.

Franck has left many comments on drawings he made all over the world and of all kinds of people. I single out two which he made on his work at the Vatican Council. The first is this:

> only very rarely have I seen a face that – fully-alive, yet without mask – showed the human in all its greatness, without a trace of falsity or pretence. It was in the face of Angelo Roncalli, better known as Pope John XXIII, that I saw this pure beauty of Spirit. He was a fat man, not handsome, but beautiful, for he was a genius of the heart, maskless.

Not everyone would have seen him that way and such seeing does not come without effort. It demands a truly religious act of attention.

> While I was in Rome [Franck continues] I often drew Cardinal Ottaviani. He fascinated me. I saw him as the Grand Inquisitor. He was no Apollo. He was old and half-blind. One eye was glassy, the other drooped. He had a confusing multiplicity of chins. As I continued drawing him I began to see him differently. Where I had only seen arrogant rigidity and decrepitude, I saw the human being – until I realised that I was seeing him with a kind of love.[7]

42

This indeed is what John's seeing amounts to. It is both the heart of his gospel and the promised land to which his Exodus journey is making its way. Before trying to grasp that as fully as possible one other point must be brought in. The words said by Jesus to Thomas, 'Blessed are those who have not seen and yet have believed,' are important here. Believing in the Fourth Gospel is always believing in rather than believing about. Its essence is believing in God in the way of Jesus Christ. Such believing means always trusting. John does not suggest that Jesus always entrusted himself to other men. He mentions a number of occasions when he actually withdrew from them because he judged that the right time for putting himself into their hands had not come. When it did come he held nothing back. It is part of the process of learning to love in parenthood, courtship, marriage, friendship and all social relations whatever, to know when and how to further the extending of trust.

This now takes us back to look again at the poetry of the Fourth Gospel. In writing and praying it not as a theological treatise nor a historical record but as a poem, John gave to his readers the most profound faith-confirming, will-moving expression of the life they were trying to live together. It was a means of interpreting their continuing experience, a rehearsal in a coherent dramatic form of what they were all committed to. We must think of it as an experience shared rather than words put together in a particular way. A poem is more than words in the sense that a meal is more than the food on the table. In both cases it is the total behaviour of the people involved that is important. It is no accident that at the heart of the life and worship of the Christian community there is a meal in and through which the behaviour, the relationships, thoughts and purposes of it are cleansed, nourished and redirected. By constant return to the table of its original institution it draws new strength, clearer sense of purpose and enlarged understanding. As in good household meals it balances silence and glad table-talk. Both have their place in furthering the life of the community large or small:

The poem is the cry of its occasion,
Part of the res itself and not about it.
The poet speaks the poem as it is,
Not as it was[8]

and our reading must do the same.

The evangelist used the Passovers of his gospel as an artist squares his paper or canvas. They serve a great many purposes, grounding his work, as we have said, in the folk-record of the Exodus and bringing it up to the moment in which Jesus eats his last meal as a man among them. Past, present and future are all brought together. In those few moments of time Jesus sums up for them the poem as it is. The imagery of the Vine and of the way to be trodden is filled out and interwoven with the promise of the advocate Spirit. The distinctive Johannine note is sounded with Jesus calling his disciples 'friends'. 'I shall not call you servants any more, because a servant does not know his master's business; I call you friends because I have made known to you everything I have learnt from my Father. You are my friends if you do what I command you.' (15:14–15).

At this most profound and revealing point of his gospel John has turned to the expression of what is fundamental to the Exodus story. Summoned, aided, guided, inspired by God, man is seeking to fulfil the Deuteronomic text, 'to love the Lord your God, to walk in all his ways'. His spiritual education lies in learning to embody in human life the ways of 'God, merciful, gracious, long-suffering, abundant in loving-kindness and faithfulness'. The word that is used to sum up the fruit of that education is friendship.

With the exception of the Society of Friends and a number of other sect churches, Christian communities have not responded to this as being the distinctive badge of their calling. That is not to say that such friendship has not flourished within them but it has tended to be eclectic and often confined to denominational lines. One has but to think that it was almost unknown until recent times for members of different denominations to pray together or even to know

44

each other though living in the same small local society, to realise to what an extent in practice the concept of friendship had been ignored. Ironically its public expression has been that conveyed by thousands of war memorials inscribed with the words of Jesus: 'Greater love hath no man than this than to lay down his life for his friends.'

Understanding of the Johannine meaning of friendship has not been made easier by the emphasis put upon sexual love in terms of romantic passion with an ever-increasing vehemence in the modern world. The two things have been set in contrast, implied in the commonplace 'just good friends' or stated in the Browning line, 'Friends, lovers that might have been'. It is love rather than friendship which occupies the attention of writers and singers and feeds the fantasies and imaginings of the majority of those who attend to them. Passionate friendship would be looked upon as much odder than sexual infatuation, passionate love would almost invariably be taken to mean a genital relationship.

It is clear that in this matter Christians and non-Christians alike have come to one of those tracts in the Exodus journey in which they have to learn how to perceive and grow into new experience of what Martin Buber called 'the inter-human'. A somewhat frantic experimentation tricked out with romanticist sentimentality is but evidence of the nagging pain of frustration. The opportunity to advance to a fuller human life presented by the greatly extended expectation of the life span of both men and women and the great gains made in knowledge of the nature of sexuality must be seen to be one of the most important spiritual disclosures of our time.

At such a time men and women are summoned to go forward beyond the relations sufficient for simply meeting the needs of everyday life – a state still very far from being realised by vast numbers throughout the world – to those which allow for more gracious and ampler relations. Understanding what Jesus Christ meant by friendship may well be the task that has now to be faced with passionate commitment by men and women and nations alike.

3

Man

What is man, that thou art mindful of him; and the son of man that thou regardest him?

Psalm 8:4

Man has very few friends in the world, certainly very few in the contemporary literature about him. The Lord in Heaven may prove to be his last friend on earth.

Abraham Heschel, *Who is Man?*[1]

I had a feeling that I was meeting for the first time an almost completely truthful man, and the experience turned out to be appropriately upsetting.

Iris Murdoch, *Under the Net* (1954)

Ernst Bloch once described the beginnings of the great religions of the world as 'impact craters'. They were the outcome and evidence of some powerful spiritual event, theophany or revelation that had at some time struck human society as a meteorite or asteroid might strike this planet. They changed the religious life of a people. They introduced new concepts by means of which men tried to understand, describe and order their life. It was because in such cases they were felt to make a great break with ways of thought and behaviour that had so far prevailed that they could be compared with a sudden almost cataclysmic event. For good and ill they changed the course of human history and the character of human lives. It is not surprising that the men who pioneered such changes were often regarded by others as subversive and dangerous people. Exile, imprisonment,

46

persecution and even death have been the experiences they have incurred. On their disciples and immediate followers some similar hardships fell until such times as the new teaching had won acceptance.

One such impact crater may be said to have been occasioned by Jesus of Nazareth. The calendar in use in a great part of the world is evidence of this. The scriptures interpreting and expounding both his teaching and what his followers believed about him have become part of the literature of many nations. The churches professing a faith in his name though by no means at one with each other none the less hail him as their Lord and Founder. The gospel with which we are concerned is itself a documentation of his impact upon the society he lived in and the movement which came into being as the outcome of that event. It was and is, as already emphasised, an interpretation designed to confirm the faith of certain groups of his followers. It was to do so by rehearsing his teaching and behaviour in respect of a way of life to be followed. It offered clues as to the ways in which the problems concerning this way should be faced and resolved. It underpinned the praying which such groups would engage in to maintain their relationship with him and with God. It flowered as the years went by in a faith in 'an almighty Saviour and a final salvation which is assured in heavenly places in Jesus Christ our Lord'. I quote the concluding words of P. T. Forsyth's book, *The Person and Place of Jesus Christ*. It was published nearly eighty years ago and fairly represented the high-watermark of a theological presentation of the gospel offering to mankind communion with God 'not through, but only in Christ and Him crucified'.

I want nevertheless to step outside such a purely theological treatment of both the gospels and the gospel. Theology may rightly be said to deal not with thoughts but with facts. They are however not the only facts that pertain to human life on earth. The human condition is a much more complex affair in which many factors operate. To gain understanding of it, that is to say, to honour the charge 'Know thyself', man must take account of the knowledge already afforded to him by innumerable sciences and by his own history. Our metaphor of the impact crater must not run away with us. Revelation is neither a purely inner experience of some person nor a self-explanatory encounter with God. It occurs in a certain social milieu shaped by circumstances whose history needs to be known. It finds expression in symbols whose meaning though known fully only to those initiated into their use calls for patient study. We have come a long way from the situation in which the Golden Bough offered a total and universal explanation of the mysteries of man's religion, but have learnt in the process to be a little more humbly perceptive.

We may begin then with the Judaism into which Jesus of Nazareth came. Our picture of this has been considerably revised and amplified by the attention now given to the work of Jewish scholars in this field. This applies not simply to the facts with which historical knowledge deals but to the understanding of them by those standing within the Jewish tradition. Modern Judaism in the matter of self-understanding may be as far from that of first-century Judaism as is twentieth-century Christianity from that of apostolic and sub-apostolic times. But there is something important in the tradition itself and felt only by those within it. The Jew is not a product of today or yesterday but of yesterday's five thousand years. There have been high and low tides of Jewish devotion, cross currents and strange whirlpools within it, but the tide is the same. If we wish to know what being a Jew meant to Jesus of Nazareth we must try to sound out its depths.

One guide to doing so may be taken from the Fourth Gospel. There is nothing in it which says that its author or his readers have ceased to be Jews. I have suggested that John's references to 'the Jews' when he is writing about opponents mean simply those who were unwilling or unable to believe that any but themselves could really be counted as Jews. Current Judaism contained any number of parties and tendencies that offered scope for such 'purer than thou' behaviour.

What is important in the Fourth Gospel in this respect is

that it repeatedly refers to Moses. He is mentioned no less than ten times. In replying to his critics in Jerusalem Jesus is said to have retorted: 'You place your hopes on Moses; I tell you that he will be your accuser before the Father because he was writing about me and you are refusing to believe what he wrote' (5:45–7). What the Mosaic writing was about was nothing other than the great redemption of the Jewish people from slavery in Egypt and the establishment of the covenanted relationship between God and them. Its announcement was in the terms of their history. It was a political event. We have to remind ourselves however that no adjective properly describes it because all such affairs, personal and social, are religious. This nation is called to be a people holy to the Lord in exactly the same sense that every pot in Jerusalem was designed and required to be so if that covenant were fulfilled. What Jesus claimed to be doing was what God had required through Moses and which the Jews were not doing now. The commission of Moses was very clear indeed. God had heard the cry of the slaves oppressed in Egypt and he therefore said: 'Come, I send you to Pharaoh to bring the sons of Israel, my people, out of Egypt' (Exod. 3:10). What the Fourth Gospel will make equally clear is that God has now sent his Son Jesus into the world that through him the world may be saved (3:17).

Hardly any word is more frequently ascribed to Jesus in the Fourth Gospel than the word 'sent'. It is meant to express the self-understanding of Jesus and of his disciples later. There is even so a special character in the role accorded to Jesus. We have noted that he claimed to have been written about by Moses. His place was solidly based. 'The Lord thy God will raise up unto thee a Prophet from the midst of thee, of thy brethren, like unto me; unto him shall ye hearken . . . I will put my words in his mouth, and he shall speak all that I command him' (Deut. 18:16–18). But at no point did Jesus openly claim to be 'that prophet', nor did John claim it on his behalf.

The reason for this is something that lies very deep in John's treatment of all questions of authority. He was living in a world where authority meant something absolute, where the population was divided between free men and slaves. Behind the sharp altercation between Jesus and the Jews set out in Chapter 8, in which certain Jews answered, 'We are descended from Abraham and we have never been slaves to anyone' (8:33), lay the dreadful truth that even before the destruction of the temple the population had been divided for almost a century between those who passively accepted Roman hegemony and in various ways tried to make the best they could for themselves, and those who in desperation fought a lengthy guerrilla war against their oppressors. Josephus himself admitted that in the time of Herod the Great 'the Jews were no longer capable of revolting against anybody'. The tale of torture and murder never ceased day by day and year by year. When the Romans under Varus returned to restore order after repeated rebellions he crucified men in thousands and sold the population of cities into slavery.

The evil of slavery in the Graeco-Roman world lay not simply in the fact that vast numbers of human beings were treated with the most brutal inhumanity but that other men justified to themselves that inhuman relationship. To do so the Greeks, so proud of free citizenship in the city-state, argued that the slave was an inferior species of being. In Israel though legally landless labourers and servants might not be enslaved but were 'hirelings' for six years, actual slavery did exist and masters could treat them as inferior beings. Along with such Hebrew hirelings went numbers of 'Canaanitish slaves' who were treated like cattle and shamefully abused. Their existence was evidence of the sick society which Israel had become and in which authority was finally represented by the infamous Herodian kings or the callous brutality of Roman officials. One may understand why the evangelist John never mentioned a Herod and treated the very word king with the utmost reserve.

What was at issue in the line taken by Jesus was something directed at the whole structure of human relationships in such a world. It touched those of sex, of family life, of rich and

poor, of learned and ignorant, of nations and military powers.
I leave to the next chapter the most basic relationship of sex,
though I would point out here that John gave it a place of
primary importance. Where the sexual relations are imma-
ture, cruel, deformed and insensitive all else in life is damaged
and stunted. What he himself had grasped of the nature of
Jesus and his work was manifest in the primacy given to love.
There is no true authority but that which originates in loving.

In that most personal setting of the room in which Jesus
shared his last meal with his friends, John gave to the other
Judas the blunt question: 'Lord, what is all this about? Do
you intend to show yourself to us and not to the world?'
(14:22). It follows the words just spoken by Jesus that
'anybody who loves me will be loved by my Father, and I
shall love him and show myself to him'. Replying to Judas,
Jesus repeated that both he and the Father would make their
home with anyone who loved him. On this learning to love the
whole course of the world's salvation would turn. Believing in
Jesus meant being committed to that.

Inseparable from it was the suffering it would entail: 'they
will expel you from the synagogues' and 'anyone who kills
you will think that he is doing God a service' (16:2). It
amounts to saying that sharing suffering is a great necessary
step forward. In the words of Sir Charles Sherrington
'altruism has to grow' and 'altruism as passion; that would
seem as yet Nature's noblest product; the greatest contribution made by man to Life'.[2] He went on to quote Keats'
recognition of this:

> 'None can usurp this height,' returned the Shade,
> 'But those to whom the miseries of the world
> Are miseries, and will not let them rest.'

The gospels were written for people living in the midst of
that sick society. They were being drawn in defiance of its
seemingly absolute power over men's lives towards a new way
of life by one who had promised them that he had overcome
that world's power. He had spoken of that life as of another
realm, eternal life or the kingdom of God. No man they had

ever known had spoken like this. No other man had shown to them such signs of a different ordering of human affairs. No one had lived it that way. Those who had followed and kept to him knew that somehow the choice had been his not theirs. Trusting him meant simply that. Who would believe that as years slipped by? How could he be kept fresh in their minds as one still amongst them. Looking back was not what they wanted. Looking into what stayed with them and grew ever more real to them was what all were in need of. The question which haunted John the writer was one which Shakespeare centuries later would face:

> Who will believe my verse in time to come,
> If it were filled with your most high deserts?
> Though yet, heaven knows, it is but as a tomb
> Which hides your life and shows not half your parts.
> If I could write the beauty of your eyes
> And in fresh numbers number all your graces,
> The age to come would say 'This poet lies!
> Such heavenly touches ne'er touched earthly faces.'[3]

It was then a great bid to get the picture right that led to this gospel being written.

How to begin it was a matter of some importance. It must be given its true religious dimension and that required those verses about the coming of the Word. It must be earthed in time and place and that meant with John the Baptist at Bethany on the far side of Jordan. It meant having a personal connection and that brought in those first disciples. The line to be followed after those things had been said had to be one that all the amazing things could be attached to and yet be simple and strong. John found it and used it quietly with the words 'the man' or 'this man'. It was not a very impressive phrase. The first occasion on which it was introduced was not any great event. 'Rabbi,' said some of John the Baptist's disciples, 'the man who was with you on the far side of the Jordan, the man to whom you bore witness, is baptizing now and everyone is going to him' (3:26). John the Baptist replied, though he had not been questioned as to what he thought

52

about it, by saying in effect that true manhood meant using whatever powers and opportunities God gave him. It was a precise description of one who was truly man. It also opened up a vista of human growth, personal and social, whose furthest reaches none could imagine. It is this which led Abraham Heschel to write: 'The Bible is not a book about God; it is a book about man,' adding, 'from the perspective of the Bible.'[4]

Very briefly we may notice how this initial lead is followed up in John's gospel. In the account of the conversation with Nicodemus the phrase 'Son of man' is repeated (3:14) and it may be presumed to be meant to designate Jesus. It is very fequently used in all the four gospels but rarely elsewhere in the New Testament. In the Fourth Gospel it is often on Jesus' lips though his critics were more concerned to know whether he claimed to be or could be known as Messiah. In one passage however (12:32) it would appear, as Geza Vermes has pointed out, that with a slight re-wording, the two titles could have been juxtaposed, that is, had Jesus said, 'When the son of man is lifted up, that is, crucified, I shall draw all men to myself.' With Messiah in mind, the crowd very naturally retorted with incomprehension. It seems likely that Jesus used son of man to designate himself. What did it mean?

For a long time Christian devotion made much of the passage in Daniel (7:13) which speaks of 'one like a son of man' who came with the clouds of heaven, and came to the Ancient of days', using it to give supernatural content to words used by Jesus. In the context of eschatological thought it provided scriptural authority for the looked-for Parousia. In relation to the earthly ministry of Jesus it gave foundation for belief in his two natures. For a great many Christians with much scholarship or none it still does, but its use is being increasingly questioned.

Where learned men disagree concerning matters in a field very far removed from that in which most of us live and read the scriptures, the best we can do to shape our understanding of such a question is to note what is said, consider the evidence and the standpoint of those who assess it, and try to relate it to our understanding of the whole gospel. The advent of Jewish scholars into the field of New Testamant studies has done much to clarify some of its difficult areas. It has opened the case for a reappraisal of what is said in the gospels in the light of, among other things, speech forms that were Aramaic. Dr Vermes has argued that in normal Aramaic usage the phrase in Daniel was not a Messianic title and 'that there is no evidence, either inside or outside the Gospels, to imply, let alone demonstrate, that "the son of man" was used as a title.'[5] I propose to stick to it as meaning 'the man' or man. I shall keep for later the title Christ.

We now have to ask who or what is man? We have to consider what it meant first of all to a first-century Jew, and secondly to ourselves today. Do the things disclosed by this man Jesus about the nature and condition of man have continuing significance nineteen centuries later? I believe that to John the matter was so important that he gave it the most dramatic expression he could. 'Jesus came out wearing the crown of thorns and the purple robe. Pilate said, "Here is the man" ' (19:5). Generations of artists have pictured the scene, for the most part with no great success. It is possibly a subject that only words and silence can express to any significant extent. Psalm 88 perhaps comes nearest to conveying the experience of it. What it means to be abhorred by God perhaps only the victims of the holocaust could begin to tell us.

Jewish reflection upon the whole subject of man had been voiced in the Psalms with a great range of feelings. The blessedness of the man whose delight is in God's law found charming likeness in the trees by the waterside. His dignity though lower than that of angels was glorious and in God he found light and joy. Enemies abounded and troubles were legion, but the man who trusted in God had every reason to hope and to sing to the Lord. What was important was the continuing scrutiny of human experience that went on. It was the search for ultimate meaning that turned it all into a learning process. The Torah provided a discipline for attaining self-knowledge through being both for the nation and for its members. It set men to search for a direction or way of living. It gave to human life as a whole the dimension of being needed or required by God in terms of righteousness and mercy, truth and love. Put in another way it provided the co-ordinates with which to chart a meaningful history for this people. It was the business of Israel's prophets to indicate in terms of public and personal behaviour how the graph read.

But 'the man' of the Fourth Gospel, possessed of that discipline of his Jewish inheritance, has stepped out of it psychologically and spiritually in order to face the problems of living in a new situation. He may be pictured as asking why the life of the Jewish people, for all its fierce violence, was manifestly unable to solve questions of national unity, just social practice, stable sexual relations and common spiritual concern. It was clear that the situation which had to be faced could not be understood and interpreted from within the thought and behaviour forms of the old order. Roman military power was still strong enough to destroy the political autonomy of peoples from Spain to Syria but it could not construct a new social order or give unified purpose to all its peoples. Its inner life had become recklessly wasteful and pointless. It could still crush dissent but it could not give new inspiration and activate new social energies. It could help the dissemination of Greek thought from city to city in all its provinces but nowhere permit new thought to challenge its economic and military power-structures. Pagan cults of worship though popular in a vast number of forms could supply no vision of life to inspire new personal initiative or common human concern.

It is unlikely that Jesus of Nazareth ever went far beyond Judaea and Galilee. He read the state of the world, nevertheless, in the city of Jerusalem. He saw his own people's troubles as part of the common sickness in which the strongest and weakest, the wisest and most foolish were all enmeshed in the length and breadth of the Roman empire. It was the salvation of the world that had become the spiritual task to which God was sending his servants. He knew himself as a man called to undertake that task. He read the signs of the times and accepted their challenge. He did so not as astrologer or an official but as an ordinary man might do, shrewdly aware of both the harsh ugliness and the hidden beauty of the terrain to be crossed. I have said already that Moses was constantly in his mind. It is equally clear that he regarded his own work as no less momentous than that of Moses. He undertook it as one to whom the covenanted relationship with God was not to be set aside but made rather the foundation and starting place of a new Exodus journey. It would be no less demanding than that march to the land of promise and inconceivable but for the assurance that God had sent him to do it. He would not turn his back upon Israel's history but raise it to a new life. The imagery, as John well knew, was appallingly accurate. The stench of corruption in Jewish life had become all too apparent.

Nowhere in the Fourth Gospel is the emphasis upon the impact of 'the man' made more pointedly than in the description of Jesus appearing in Jerusalem at the time of the feast of Tabernacles (ch. 7). It was a time of rejoicing for the fruits of the earth and the life-giving water. The evangelist set the scene as one of expectation on the part of the assembled crowds. 'People stood in groups whispering about him' for the temple police were among them too. 'Some said, he is a good man; others, no, he is leading the people astray.' When Jesus appeared in the temple he challenged his hearers: 'Why do you want to kill me?' He took up the disputed cure of the sick man on the Sabbath which had already been judged offensive. Was it not life-giving just as much as circumcision, and like circumcision to be given priority over the rule of the Sabbath? His boldness attracted further notice: 'Is not this "the man" they want to kill? Among the crowd many were openly saying, "When the Christ comes, will he give more signs than this man?" ' (7:31). Even the temple police returning empty-handed to the chief priests and Pharisees protested, 'Never man spake like this man' (7:46).

I am suggesting that in putting this emphasis upon 'the man' John was withstanding the temptation and the tendency

56

to over-theologise and over-institutionalise the person of
Jesus. He could not but be aware of the brilliance of theological learning and acumen with which Paul had presented
the figure and work of Jesus the Christ to both Jews and
Gentiles. Perhaps he recognised that Paul was already a European in a way that he himself could not be. Paul was right
in affirming that 'there is neither Jew nor Greek, neither bond
nor free, neither male nor female, for all are one in Christ
Jesus' (Gal. 3:28) but was it not the idealism of the European
mind that was at work, already divorcing the theory from the
actual behaviour? Had not Paul himself confessed to the split
in his own personal life, to the war in his members to be ended
only when the last trumpet sounded, to the very absence of
unity within man himself? I am suggesting that John because
of his Jewishness was more reluctant to devise a theology to
account for God's dealings with man, choosing rather to dwell
on what had appeared in human terms in the man Jesus
which were none the less the glory, the grace and the truth
of the Father.

In the second place he was reserved about institutions. He
knew that even among twelve men there could be discussion
as to who was the greatest. He knew that some men yearned
for authority and others welcomed it for not very good
reasons. Becoming a larger community meant that buildings
and regulations, organisation and job-direction would be
needed. We shall look at this later in considering the Johannine church. What John was chiefly concerned with was the
still greater need to keep alive the original relationship which
they had had in the presence of Jesus, the relationships which
that man had brought into being. In them lay the soul of the
movement. What would it profit the church if it gained the
whole world and lost that? In the figure of Jesus the servant
they had been shown the true image of human/divine personal
life. In years to come if they turned away from it and accepted
some other figures as more desirable for worldly life, would
they not need to recall his words: 'Why do you go about to
kill me?'

All this raises one important question. Does the Fourth

Gospel tell us what Jesus gave to the first Christian communities that would be sufficient to equip them to become and continue to be the leaven of the world's salvation process? Does it indicate what they were to do in the political world or in the arts, the economy, the sciences of human society?

That the Christian church has been ambivalent about such things is evident in its history. At times it has played the patron to the arts, fostered learning and inspired political thought as well as coming to terms with a variety of polities. At others it has renounced these things as snares or shrunk from contamination by them, counselling men and women not to touch pitch. Criticism of Jesus in this respect has been sharp and severe. 'The great prophet of the soul left out of his mission the traditional food of the soul. Music, poetry, painting, philosophy, science, counted nought for the salvation of man.'

Reference to the soul is not common in the Fourth Gospel. It appears rather strangely in the short discourse (12:23–28) as a quotation from Psalm 42 and a recollection of the Synoptic accounts of the agony in the Garden of Gethsemane, which otherwise has no place in John's story. What we have in John is something more important which can best be described as a conception of the person and the personal. What this gospel says to all men and women who make up the world is: 'Love one another as I have loved you' or, put in another way, 'go about your life as those who are loved'.

There is no attempt to describe the lover or loving such as found treatment in the Romantic literature of Europe. On the other hand this gospel shifts all our attention from thought to action. It is divine action God's giving his Son for the world's salvation, which underlies the whole story. This in turn becomes the action of Jesus in seeking out men and women whom he draws into a loving relationship. Its end-term is living (and if need be dying) for others. The new society, indicated in the gospel and the Johannine epistles as 'we', embodies this act of loving by establishing a community of persons. The word for them will be long in coming because it would need long experience and much failure to bring home to those involved what was really at stake. It proved easier for Christians to think and speak lengthily of the Persons of the Godhead than to envisage human society in terms of persons. It was in some sense a measure of the extent to which 'the man' of the Fourth Gospel was obscured by the hierarchical imagery so dear to the Roman political mind. What were lost to sight in the processes of ecclesiastical organisation were the radical relationships that obtained where two or three were gathered together. As the numbers of adherents to the Christian communities grew was it possible to retain the spirit and character of the personal relations they had once known?

The problem was intensified as we can see from the Acts of the Apostles and the Pauline epistles by matters of ordinary social welfare. Roman society had built up in the great cities a monstrous system of 'bread and circuses' to feed and amuse its armies of men and women whose citizenry had lost its meaning, whose economy based on slave labour lurched towards disaster. How would Christians feed the hungry and care for the sick? The man Jesus had done these things in spectacular fashion. He had challenged his friends to consider how the multitudes should be fed. They could not but recall the prophetic command, 'See thou deal thy bread to the hungry.' Attempting to do so in Jerusalem for the widows of their own community they ran into difficulties which led to the appointment of the Seven (Acts 6). The Twelve were left free to pray and to preach. Organisation has begun to meet such demands.

We know too little about the daily life of those small groups of Christians to say how well or otherwise they coped with such growing problems in detail or the overall matter of an alternative social and economic order. The gospel itself gives no clues beyond pointing to the works which Jesus did and his insistence upon his words being life-giving. It recalled the most startling words: 'I am the bread of life' and 'the bread I shall give for the life of the world is my flesh' (6:51). The Jews very understandably retorted, 'How can this man give us his flesh to eat?' The question remains with us still.

What did 'the man' do? The symbols employed in the story of the feeding of the multitude are clear. There are limited resources but responsibility must be accepted and common action taken. Waste is to be avoided. An attempt to hasten the end by making this man king had to be avoided. The 'political connotation', as Geza Vermes calls it, inseparable not simply from Galilean conditions but from all human society, had to be faced and accepted but not in the short-term programmes of Zealotry. The kingdom of God for whose coming the Christian communities waited and worked must have its own times of growth. Those who hungered for it must in patience possess their souls, make mistakes but learn from them in penitence and trust, and above all remain attentive to the Spirit. They must not lose sight of the pattern of true human relationships which they had been introduced to by this man. Tested day after day by every conceivable problem they must learn how it could be extended to become universal. Their praying must be the channel through which the growth of the Spirit-led community proved its fitness for the tasks put before it.

Jesus did not promise the immediate solution to all human problems but spoke rather of tribulations to be faced. What he did teach his friends was that they should not be afraid of the future and refuse to make changes in their behaviour that gave practical shape to developing life. They must not dissociate their thought from practice or say what they did not do. Above all they must not deny the potential unity of the person and the community of mankind. 'This man' had put this before them as the very heart of his final prayer among them, 'that they may be one, even as thou, Father, art in me, and I in thee' (17:21). It was no blurred pantheistic picture of life but an exact statement of its essential nature. The otherness of God is the only true guarantee of man's freedom to grow to his true spiritual stature. The love of God is the energy at work to draw him into a true relation with God. In its turn that becomes the pattern of human life, a respect for the otherness of all men and women, a love which is a concern to draw them into relations which confirm them

as persons. Claude Lévi-Strauss has said what that means,
albeit in negative terms, when he confessed that in the streets
of Calcutta he did not dare look anyone in that terrible crowd
in the eye 'for the sheer satisfaction of establishing contact
with another human being'.[6] A woman of great Christian
faith has shown that it can be done.

I have suggested that at a like moment in human history
a man did precisely that. He looked men and women, Jews,
Samaritans, Greeks and Romans, learned and ignorant,
friendly and hostile, in the eye to make contact with them as
human beings, as potential friends. He drew a few of them
to himself to embody that way of living so that it might under
God be the way forward for mankind. It required of them a
great act of believing in him because for the moment there
was little to show for it but tribulation and pain and death.
The evangelist John understood what it meant not any better
perhaps than some few named and many more nameless men
and women did, but in a way that he could put into words.
He did that because he was a poet and that is a poet's job.

What we have then in his gospel is something more relevant
to the needs of mankind than almost anything that has been
written, though we have to turn it into praying to read it
aright. It was never more needed than now when the world's
population lives under the threat of annihilation or perversion
of all that is human. 'When a great ideal', wrote Lancelot
Whyte, 'has ceased to illuminate the human understanding
and has therefore lost its power, man has no choice but to
search afresh for some element in the processes of the real
world with which he can identify himself.'[7] That element
today is that which was being disclosed to the world in the
man Jesus. As yet the great bulk of mankind has failed either
to see him or to identify itself with him. Perhaps, as it was
once a woman who exclaimed, 'Come see a man . . . can this
be the Christ?' it may be that a woman's voice has now to
be heard.

4

Woman

Women need a favoring wind.
Gerald Sykes, *The Hidden Remnant* (1962)

In the bankruptcy of reason, she alone was real.
Henry Adams, *Mont St Michel and Chartres* (1913)

We saw for a moment, laid out among us the body of the complete human being, whom we have failed to be but at the same time, cannot forget. All that we might have been we saw.
Virginia Woolf, *The Waves* (1931)

In the Letter of the Churches of Vienne and Lyons, describing the cruel martyrdoms suffered by many Christians in AD 177, there is a notable sentence. It says that those who witnessed them 'saw during the contest, even with the eyes of flesh, in the person of their sister, Him who was crucified for them, to assure those who believed on Him that everyone who suffereth for the glory of Christ hath for ever fellowship with the living God'.[1] The brief testimony to St Blandina deserves to be better known. It says very plainly and simply that those witnesses to that terrible event saw Jesus Christ in a woman. She is sharing for ever a fellowship in the divine.

Hers was not however a time favourable to appreciation of that remarkable vision. Our own is scarcely more prepared to welcome it, though more uneasy about appearing not to do so. The reason for this lies in the matter of power which by longstanding tradition belongs to men. Authority resided in the male in the social structures of the ancient world. Pagan, Jewish and Christian thought was at one in such a

62

matter. The advent of the modern world did not greatly change the prevailing mode of thinking and behaviour. Its most remarkable feature, an unparalleled development of technology, went far to reinforce the view that in every sphere of life it was the possession of power that really counted. By dint of tools and organisation man was the master of things.

The lure of such Faustian possession of power has been almost overwhelming. Its successes are patent and self-advertised. Every day it can demonstrate new achievements. It has none the less been haunted by a growing awareness of its vulnerability, of the absence of self-knowledge and common human concern that could arrest the fear that men's skills were adding to rather than solving the problems of life on the planet. Two prophet-poets, Goethe and Blake, who stood on the threshold of modern times, pointed out where attention must be directed. Goethe called her Marguerite, Blake 'the eternal female' under a variety of names. What was missing from and being avoided in this vast intricate power-structured world was womanhood. It could be amusingly referred to in Shavian terms in the lament of Professor Higgins: 'Why can't women be like men?' More seriously it could be phrased as a warning. 'If Man's relationship to Nature', wrote Karl Stern, 'is nothing but that of a technological victory, it amounts to a loveless union of Man and Nature, a rape, and will end in perdition.'[2] Our tomorrows would signify nothing but sound and fury, our conquests of nature fill our mouths with no more than dust unless and until womanhood be admitted to its true function in human life. Since the male-structured world had as yet given little attention to what this might be beyond bearing men's children and in particular sons, it could not be easy for either men or women to come up with satisfactory answers. Sexual relations quite stubbornly and demonically refused to become so restricted to a kind of mechanical function. The most searing and self-destructive experience of sexuality as such may be found put in words in Tolstoy's Kreutzer Sonata story. It told the world brilliantly what a century later would be written large in the much publicised sexual experiences of our times. D. H.

Lawrence described them as crucifixion. John Cowper Powys called them torture. Less extreme observations do exist but no one could contemplate contemporary society without feeling misgivings about it.

Our concern is what bearing the Fourth Gospel has on this matter. I suggest that almost alone among first-century Christian writing it points to the part which womanhood must occupy in the reshaping of human life which metaphorically is called being born again. Since women are those who give birth to human beings it might have led men to consider with some care what part in or contribution to birth they actually gave. On the whole they preferred not to do so. They assumed that the woman's part was that of providing fertile ground for the male seed. There until recent times the matter was left. Almost all that was said about women was written by men, few of whom, if we may for the moment take a woman's view of them, had the slightest knowledge of what they presumed to talk about. 'What a hopeless thing a man's consciousness was,' wrote Dorothy Richardson. 'How awful to have nothing but a man's consciousness.'[3] Lest we think that is too partial a judgment we might bear in mind that as late as 1889 English judges ruled that the word person in English statutes did not include women. Practice made clear what this could mean in social life. For all but a very few it meant suffering inflicted upon women quite simply because they were legally and socially weaker than men. To be so disadvantaged in a world where the power game is judged to be all-important is to be at the mercy of those who will win. The allotting of spoils – 'to every man a damsel or two' – may have changed some of its forms, but the overall outcome has remained much the same both in Christian and other societies until very recent times. To be born of a woman is a plain fact, to be born a woman has been for the most part a misfortune.

Our modern world has increasingly been faced by evidence of great rifts in human relations, made evident in violence and fearful in anticipation. These include colour and class conflict, Super Power rivalry measured in terms of weaponry, ideological militancy, inner-city life marked by bitter frustration, hopelessness bred by continuing unemployment. Interlocked with all these is that of the relations between men and women. It may well be the most fundamental of all. It must certainly compel re-examination by Christians of the way they have expressed their belief in God and their understanding of human life. It may well require them to ask, as Rosemary Ruether has done, whether the maleness of Jesus has any ultimate significance. It may confront them with discomforting words about the imagery of God's Fatherhood. Mary Daly has stated quite tersely, 'if God is male then male is God', and gone on to dissociate herself from the Jewish-Christian tradition because it has been for so long the foundation of patriarchal society in the West and the source of much idolatrous male imagery. In her view it is not possible to use the word God free from the hateful suggestiveness of male dominance, aggression and rape. She has not been alone in making this forthright challenge. There are many who now question God-imagery presented in terms of absolute power who sympathise with her.

That Jewish-Christian tradition has none the less some ambiguous features. The role of women, good wives or harlots, is in the Old Testament record not without importance. To find a wife is undeniably to find a good thing! There is a much more important level than this to be reached in recognising with Franz Rosenzweig that 'the Song of Songs is the focal book of revelation'.[4] Human love exists because God loves: 'the Song of Songs was an "authentic", that is, a "worldly" love lyric; precisely for this reason, not in spite of it. It was a genuinely "spiritual" song of the love of God for man.' It was here that too many men stumbled. They could not perceive the very worldliness of God nor realise that matrimony was 'infinitely more than love' since they had grown up in a culture that had torn apart God and man. Christians fared little better in spite of the glimpse they had during the first days of the church of a quite new relationship of the sexes. It is clear from the New Testament that women played an important part in shaping the new communities of

Christians, as St Paul willingly admitted. He was greatly indebted to them and at one point ready to dismiss the sexual distinction. From that position he later retreated and in his most authoritative manner insisted on their subordination to men. He insisted that they should be silent because theirs was a secondary role and woman herself the primal transgressor. At no far distant time such sexual repudiation would harden into an ecclesiastical system and fill the world with a tradition of sexual guilt.

We have seen none the less from the story of St Blandina that the great wall was not without breaches. By sheer force of spiritual integrity the many Catherines, Margarets, Elizabeths and Teresas claimed along with a Hilda, a Clare and a Joan a place in the saintly communion. Communities of both men and women ruled over by an abbess were not unknown. A special place of honour came in time to be given to the mother of Jesus though Marian feasts and hymns only came into existence after the Council of Ephesus in AD 431. The city which had once for so long venerated the virgin goddess Diana accorded to Mary the title 'Theotokos'. Thereafter the floodtide of human imagination was loosed in her name but it was not until the time of the crusades that she began, as Henry Adams remarked, 'to overshadow the Trinity itself'. The Cistercian Order, founded in 1098, 'from the first put all its churches under the special protection of the Virgin while guildsmen and warriors vied with each other in according to her their utmost devotion'.[5] Financial investment and art together saluted her queenly dignity, making palaces of her cathedrals and lyrical ecstasies of her hymns:

Salve, Mater Salvatoris!
Vas electum! Vas honoris!
Vas coelestis Gratiae!

From then onwards it continued with frequent renewals until the supreme honour of her Assumption into heaven was acknowledged. In English verse it found its expression in D. G. Rossetti, saluting her:

Now sitting fourth beside the Three
Thyself a woman Trinity –
Being a daughter born to God
Mother of Christ from stall to rood,
And wife unto the Holy Ghost.

Notwithstanding all this, its bearing upon the status and treatment of women was doubtful. The Christian world could with some justice be described as 'a half-world in which the feeling and the symbolically feminine' remained unassimilated. Perhaps the oddest of all ultra-romantic musing upon womanhood appeared in Ruskin's lecture, 'Of Queen's Gardens', delivered in Manchester in 1864. It contains the remarkable statement that 'Shakespeare has no heroes; he has only heroines'. It demanded for girls the same opportunities for education as for boys with a warning against them touching theology! It spoke lengthily on woman's part in the life of the commonwealth without venturing to examine the economic and legal conditions that governed their lives. Not inexplicably his encounter with womanhood in marriage was from the outset a disaster. It is difficult to escape the conclusion that the two evil legacies of the failure of Christendom to treat women as persons of equal dignity with that of men, which resulted on the one hand in the hatred and contempt from the times of the Fathers until that of Schopenhauer and Strindberg, and on the other in the false romanticism from the Troubadours to Ruskin and the Pre-Raphaelites, were equally poisonous. Neither of them is quite dead today both within and outside the churches.

Such attitudes towards women affected not only the relations of the two sexes but the theology of the church. Dorothée Sölle has described it as being 'unaware of the emotions' and 'insensitive to what people experience'. To deprecate or lose sight of the feminine is to weaken the sense of the relatedness which must lie at the heart of a religious sense of reality, the truth of which is set out in the Johannine account of what Jesus said at the last supper with his disciples. The imagery used by Jesus throughout his teaching whether in materials like bread, wine and water or in the actions of shepherding, serving and feeding is that which highlights relationships and dependency. It rests upon what Karl Stern has called 'the unspeakable mystery of the "and" – of God *and* his creation, of God *and* his people, of Christ *and* his Church'. It enters human life most significantly in sexuality since 'the sexual and, of man *and* woman, is a reflection of the others. All being is nuptial.'[6] It is for this reason that the Fourth Gospel sums up the truth of such relatedness in terms of loving. It omits the familiar imagery of the ruler and servants, the judge and the punished, the despot and the obedience he exacts, all of which belonged to the male conception of governance and power, and all of which beget fears of being questioned and displace trust by an anxiety to please. What is really at issue in this is not so much whether the name and pronouns used for God are masculine but whether the active relationship between God and his people is that which primarily expressed the truth that God's only power is that of loving. To learn what that means both sexes have to learn afresh what the feminine in human life expresses.

Re-reading the Fourth Gospel with this in mind means two things today. It must make us aware of what part in the story John gave to women. It must also require us to attend to what women themselves are saying today about it, to what questions they are putting to the whole Church, to what changes they are calling for in human affairs. As Mary Collins has said, 'Ahead for most of the Church, for its theological leaders and its bishops as well as its members, is the awareness that the problem is not women at all but patriarchy and andocentrism,'[7] A book like *In Memory of Her*, by Elisabeth Schüssler Fiorenza (1983), should be not only an indispensable guide to such re-reading but recognised as indicative of a new consciousness transforming our outlook upon spiritual life. A great artist is an androgynous creature and both aspects of his or her work demand our attention.

In almost half the deeply dramatic scenes of the Fourth Gospel women play a distinctive part. In the first of these at the wedding at Cana the mother of Jesus is introduced somewhat strangely by going unnamed but addressed as Woman. It has frequently been asserted that this was not unusual but it grates on our ears and provokes a question. Its tone is a very long way from that used in a Talmud story quoted by Israel Abrahams in his lectures on the Glory of God (Shekinah): 'When Rabbi Joseph heard the nearing footsteps of his mother, he stood up and said, "I will arise before the Glory of God which approaches." '[8] I note further that Elisabeth Schüssler Fiorenza says firmly that 'we have no precedent in Jewish or Graeco-Roman sources for a son to address his mother as "woman" '. Why then did John put it that way? Why did he use words that sound a note of rejection? I believe that in all such presentations of people the evangelist combined their historical character with the mythical so that they represent in personal forms the much larger issues of life and death. In the story to which the words 'the first sign' were attached something of primary importance is to be looked for. It concerns nothing less than the death of an old community and the birth of a new one. It has not yet taken place because the hour of the death of Jesus and his rebirth in the life of the community of the Spirit is yet to come but the process of disengagement has its beginning here. Sexuality, so deeply important in human life, is neither the beginning nor the end. There was life before sexuality appeared and there will be life that transcends it. The family though profoundly important is likewise not the be-all nor end-all of human relationships. It too must die and be freed from genealogical restrictions. The Jesus who said 'Call no man father' implied as much, 'Call no woman mother', and very abruptly in the Matthean story declared that to love father *or* mother more than himself was unworthy of him. Only life in the new community can bring human beings to their true fulfilment. 'The law of blood is transposed into an elective communion of brothers and sisters.' So the first sign points forward to the final achievement when the new form brought into being by the Spirit will have entered human history. All that womanhood can under God contribute to it will be gathered up and be made channel of yet greater grace. Something more than compassionate provision for Mary was being made when her son dying on the cross commended her to the keeping of that disciple whom he loved.

Yet the choice of a wedding as the first sign-pointer towards the new life made it clear that it was not to be sexless but with sexual relations transformed. It was told in challenging fashion:

> The bride has passed into the hall,
> Red as a rose is she:
> Nodding their heads before her goes
> The merry minstrelsy[9]

which is how it should have been told perhaps, but not in John's account of it. From first to last there is no mention of the bride. Now it is undeniable that men's motives in marriage have ranged from the very basest to the most exalted, but all of them presumably had a woman in view. They might adore her, despise her, buy her or bully her but they could not altogether ignore her. Why then did John leave her out? The short answer is that he saw her and meant others to see her as a non-person, or simply a woman-shaped blank that men would fill in as they thought fit to do. What she might be in herself they were not greatly concerned to know. She was desirable as an object to be possessed. Fifteen centuries later in his play *Much Ado about Nothing* Shakespeare made much the same point. It turns on the current pronunciation of Nothing as noting. Claudio has noted Hero as a desirable object. He has not really seen her as a person, as a woman to be related to or sought with understanding and love. It is his own expectations that excite him. When these are dashed he turns instantly against her and is wholly concerned with his own injured self. We may hear the same tones in Torvald's voice in Ibsen's *Doll's House* generations later.

A matter of such importance does not go away when ignored. It is evident from the Synoptic gospels that Jesus was frequently questioned about marriage and divorce. He is said to have repeated the words of Genesis describing the two partners to the sexual union becoming one flesh and to have firmly rejected the idea that marital relations would in the resurrection life still obtain. Both Jewish and Christian writings of the time exhibit considerable diversity of views, some seeking to maintain the stability afforded by the patriarchal pattern, some in view of a conceivable end of the world adopting a stricter ascetic line. What the wedding at Cana story was meant to make clear was that marriage could be the channel of opportunity for both sexes to learn what loving meant. The truth about what was actually happening is blurted out by the older woman because she has seen it all happen before. The male-dominated society has too limited a view of what is needed. It has not tried to learn from woman's love what it discloses of God's relationship to human beings. In Mark Rutherford's words, 'In the love of a woman to the man who is of no account, God has provided us with a true testimony of what is in his own heart.'[10] It is not the final picture of the love of God and there can be a point where it is misused. The egotism of the couple or the family can be as deadly as any other form of individualism. But John's story is a sad realistic assessment of what has been done to marriage hitherto, depriving it of that abundance of good wine that it could provide for successive stages of life. It is not the only field of education in which humanity has acted in crudely mechanical ways and failed as yet to enable men and women to learn the truth about themselves and others but it is for most of us the most important, which is why John gave it its place of priority.

In the story of the Samaritan woman the artistry of the evangelist is still more clearly displayed. She is the very reverse of the woman-shaped blank. In the male-dominated world she is indomitable. She has learned how to hold her own. Symbolically she is the drawer of water, mater and materia, the ocean from which life and love have sprung. In herself as a person she is quick-witted, resourceful, defensive and if need be deceitful. She has established a relationship with men which is not simply 'and'; it has with some practice become that of 'but'. No other conversation in the Fourth

Gospel has the same give and take character as this. Pure invention on John's part it may be but its significance is overwhelming. Here is the first truly apostolic figure called into being by Jesus, a Samaritan and a woman.

It is when we are introduced to the named women of this gospel that their contribution to the understanding of what Jesus did is more firmly defined. A human household for a moment is happily revealed – 'Jesus loved Martha and her sister and Lazarus' – but the shadow of death has been cast upon it. Death as a fact in living is being taken into the story and John chose to do this through women. Men have no doubt attached to it either brutal matter-of-factness or a mystical dimension. It has fallen to women to take death into the daily task of living. It is right that they should be those through whom the first steps are taken to grasp death with loving and trustful hands.

So Martha goes out to meet Jesus as one not doubting that she is loved, as one both sorrowful and expectant, reproachful and humbly patient. She can speak plainly about it. She meets the challenge that Jesus puts to her by simply admitting that she believes him to be the Christ, the Son of God, who was to come into the world. The phrase is one often to be repeated. What we want to know is its content, the nature in fact of the Johannine gospel. John did not choose to insert a theological discourse at this point nor refer to a life in another world. He spoke rather of resurrection through belief in Jesus, through relationship with him that partook of that which obtained between God and himself. It offered no explanation of death such as the Pauline epistles assert. The test is entirely personal: 'Do you believe this?' where this means the awesome relationship with God, and Martha accepts it. As Elisabeth Moltmann-Wendel has said of her: 'John throws overboard our traditional image of Martha; he restores to life the aggressive, disturbing, sage, active Martha who went against all the conventions, mistress of the house, housewife, apostle, the woman who stands beside Peter in her own right'.[11] Hers is a Henry Moore figure with 'anxiety held in check' and her witness is as robustly lucid:

72

She testifies to that first truth
The hour-glass cannot hold.
Her voice recalls the voice of Ruth
When she to Naomi told
A pledge too dear for time to break
Or earth to render vain;
Dark is the radiance doomed to wake
This Danaë to the rain.[12]

Medieval hagiography pictured her as dragon-slayer but it was the oddly perceptive Meister Eckhart who, having recognised how the evangelist John had penetrated the depths of the divine mysteries, preached upon Martha and boldly proclaimed that hers was the more mature spiritual response than that of her sister, marvelling at what was displayed in her. 'Understanding and being understood, seeing and being seen, holding and being held; that is the last stage where the Spirit perseveres in rest, united to beloved eternity.'[13] In the many movements of late medieval spirituality that produced women of profound wisdom and great grace it was to the figure of Martha that so many turned.

The portrait of Mary of Bethany lacks nothing of full recognition of her part in the story but follows an independent line. John did not repeat the Lukan comment that when Jesus came as a guest to the home in Bethany she chose to sit at his feet, because he had already pictured her going out hastily to fling herself before him overcome with weeping for her dead brother. In her grief Jesus shared to the full, to the amazement of others who were present. The Fourth Gospel leaves its readers in no doubt that loving and suffering pain and grief are inextricably bound together. No less than joy sorrow has its due place in life. Who shall say how much this woman who anointed Jesus with such care helped to prepare him as a man to face the death that he was to go forward to so soon just as he in turn helped them to grow through the stages of near despair to a trust in God that envelops death. In this final sign-story before the putting to death of Jesus, John made symbol and parable go as far they could. They tell us nothing of resurrection life save that love sustains whatever meaning it can have. They are not meant to forestall the death on the cross with an assurance that death could not take him away but to turn the reader's attention to something which was shown in the life, death and resurrection of Jesus Christ, that is to say that the power of God is nothing else but the power of loving. Against the reality of the meaninglessness, futurelessness and powerlessness that such a possibility or probability as annihilation by nuclear warfare holds out to mankind, it maintains a trust in such loving.

It was to show how that can be expressed that one other woman was needed in this story's unfolding; one woman alone who was greeted by name by Jesus. She appears late in the narrative as one who stood with the Lord's mother and Mary the wife of Cleopas at the foot of the cross. To identify Mary of Magdala rightly she should be disengaged from the legend of the great sinner that crept into art and literature by confusing two incidents in St Luke's gospel and one concerning an unnamed woman in St Mark. Her part is too important to be even so slightly mistaken. She should hold her unique position quite clearly as the first witness to the risen Christ, the first bearer of apostolic commission, and being in person for some hours the confessing church on earth. Hers is the voice that speaks through the ages with tender concern and uninhibited joy for Jesus Christ's sake. In the course of the Fourth Gospel we come a long way from the unnamed and unnoticed bride of the first story to this Mary greeted by the risen Christ and it is unlikely that John wanted it otherwise. 'Nothing', wrote Conrad, 'can beat a woman for a clear vision of reality.' How much the church has in fact suffered from failing or being unwilling to recognise this is something to be reflected upon. Why, one may wonder, when St Paul so confidently rehearsed to the Christians in Corinth the list of the witnesses to the resurrection and included himself did he omit her name? Must we really accept a statement that suggests that in so great a cloud of witnesses not one woman found a place? Does it not rather compel us to look more closely at the distortion of Christian witness that has marred and weakened the life of the church by this suppression of the testimony of women to such an extent? Mention has been made of those confessors and martyrs who found a place in the calendar of the saints, but of the continuing presence of the woman in the life of the church if we ask, 'And what's her history?' the answer has been supplied: 'A blank, my lord.' It was not that she was unable or unwilling to tell of her love but that the male-ordered church was unprepared to listen. We cannot know how many voices were stifled by fear of exciting male hatred, but we can reflect upon the thinking that reduced Mary of Magdala's name to the contemptuous maudlin and excited the frenzied witch-burning that swept through so-called Christian communities when religious zeal was most intense. It was a small thing no doubt that the commemoration of St Mary Magdalene which had its place in the first Prayer Book of Edward VI should have been removed from the second, but it showed how reformers were minded to think of women.

To the evangelist John, Mary Magdalene was not only a witness to resurrection but the bearer of a message. It is of great importance in the Johannine understanding and presentation of the gospel. It replaces the visual expression of the ascension of Jesus by a few words and places it prior to any appearances of the figure of Jesus to the disciples. It followed a curt phrase that prohibited touching or clinging to him and a little later will be reinforced by an equally sharp comment on the happiness of those who believe though they have not shared in the experience of seeing him. John was writing to the growing number of Christians who had not been present in those first days of the Easter experience. If a late dating of this gospel is accepted the events of those days could have been no more than a few memories, more likely to kindle fantasies than to underpin faithful living. That appearances had a place in the early tradition of the church is undeniable. Whether they were more than partly symbols of devotion and partly products of pious imagination is matter for conjecture. The appearance of Jesus in the Apocryphal Gospels and many books of Acts are evidence of the bizarre lengths to which the

75

latter could go. What John was concerned to do was to free belief in the presence of the Spirit given to the church by Jesus from dependence upon such things no matter how reliable an authority could be quoted to support them. Resurrection was something to be experienced in the day to day living of the disciples. 'We know that we have passed from death to life because we love the brethren.' It was too real a matter of present relationships to need substantiation from appearances or even scriptural authority. It would contradict the whole burden of John's gospel to direct the believer's attention backwards. The trust and the love with which he was most concerned needed no such authorisation.

No other gospel gives such attention to personal relationships, to the truth that our relation to God is that which shows itself in our relation to fellow human beings. Resurrection comes late in the narrative but it comes as something prepared for step by step in the uncovering of the relationship Jesus had with his disciples. Much of it they very plainly did not understand until at and after his death. Then, as Stanley Spencer said of his pictures of resurrection, what was evident was 'the passing of the state of non-realisation of the possibilities of heaven in this life to a sudden awakening to that fact'. Men and women were caught up into a new kind of life of which Jesus had told them and brought them into. It was realisation of what Joel's prophecy had spoken: 'I will pour out my Spirit upon all flesh, and your sons and your daughters shall prophesy.' The relationships of worldly power would give place to those of agape and the daughters would take their place as of right in the new community of the Spirit.

It is with the task laid upon both sexes to bring into being such a right relationship that the church and humanity as a whole are fundamentally concerned. John used the word agape to denote it and his gospel is the first great Christian declaration of its nature. Agape had long been in use in the Septuagint to denote God's love for his people and the love which they were commanded to show to him and to their neighbours, a thing we have very tardily begun to see that we cannot do if we hate ourselves. It is possible that the

76

choice of this word by John and other New Testament writers
may have been influenced by the desire to avoid the pagan
associations of the word eros. The increasing Greek read-
ership of the gospel would be familiar with many aspects of
eros in contemporary culture ranging from the fierce sensual
passion to the purified direction of the soul towards the divine
expounded by Plato and other philosophers. But he was
writing not for the wise and learned nor even for the citizenry
of contemporary society but for numbers of all sorts and
conditions of men and women summoned to engage in
building a wholly new kind of life of which the negatives
'neither Jew nor Greek, bond nor free, male nor female' gave
a startling if inadequate description. The sexual was but one
feature of both the old life and the new but it was of fundamental importance. We have already seen that in failing to
withstand the temptation to accept patriarchal authori-
tarianism in both domestic and ecclesial life the Christian
church committed itself to structures which went far to
pervert the relationships which it talked about but failed to
honour. In matters of sex it did not prove to be any more
enlightened but rather retreated from the opportunity
glimpsed in its earliest days of drawing out in actual living
the implications of the belief that God had taken the flesh of
humanity as his body making it holy. What sadly becomes
evident in Paul's treatment of women's part in the life of the
church is his inability to overcome a deep distrust of sexuality
and a fear that women's freedom to express themselves uncon-
trolled by men must bring chaos into human relations. 'It is
a good thing for a man to have nothing to do with women.'
Whatever is connected with sex is dangerous and to be
avoided. Safety – and Paul rarely envisages a more positive
relationship than this – therefore lies in the domestic seclusion
of women, strict control of their dress and subordination to
male authority. The sins of the flesh to which women are the
temptresses are those most defiling. Other sins are 'outside
the body', those of sex defile the Lord's temple which is the
body. He went on to allow a prophylactic marriage without
ever supposing that it was a final insult to women.

77

It was to leave a disastrous legacy to centuries to come. It severed the connection between eros and agape, set sacred and profane love at war on each other, made the life of spiritual perfection that of celibacy, and brought into being great numbers of Gnostic heresies which made absolute the distinction between spirit and matter. It has with some modifications lasted until our own times. Anders Nygren's book *Agape and Eros* (1983) insisted that the collision between them was 'Christianity's hour of destiny'. Agape was a totally different kind of love from anything known to the pagan world. Human values had no place in it whatever. It is identified entirely with the nature of God and such experience as man has of agape is the outflowing of the agape of God. At first sight it would appear to be the Johannine gospel in all its purity and power.

Two things refute this. There are in the first place passages in the Fourth Gospel and the Epistles which speak of loving the world contrasted with loving God yet using agape for both, and again using it to describe the love which men had for each other and for Jesus himself in contrast to the universal love that should flow from the agape of God. Much more important however is the human experience of Christians which has refused to be bound by the theoretical distinction and gradually forced recognition of the need to bring eros and agape together. It is this which underlies the long struggle to bring men and women together as joint heirs of the grace of God and to give to their sexual relations a sacral dignity. Grace is given not to oust or subdue nature represented by eros but to bring it to perfection. For too many centuries Christians looked at life through the filters of doctrine that obscured and distorted their views of the body and their sexuality. They were largely unready to learn from each other the truth about themselves and nowhere more unwilling to do so than in the relations of men and women. Education as a life process which is far wider and more profound than literacy can afford us was but fitfully admitted. It could and did gather recognition by escaping from theological control and finding channels for itself in the arts and sciences.

The most obvious example is to be seen in the literature devoted to love, and notably in the novel. John Bayley's study of this in *The Characters of Love* says that 'the best as well as the worst imaginative writing is still largely about love – for everyone recognises that, whatever you call it, sexual love is for most people the most interesting and memorable aspect of life. It is with this kind of love – eros rather than agape – that literature is most concerned.'[14] If that is true it represents the most powerful reason for the rejection of or indifference to a Christianity committed to agape so understood by growing numbers of people. It is because I believe that it is a misrepresentation of John's understanding of agape that I regard the Fourth Gospel as that book in the New Testament which has the most to say to our times. The place that John gave in it to women was the basis upon which a new understanding of agape could be built. Without it sexual love would be for ever made a rival or an enemy to the divine love whereas what John was making way for was the very opposite of that. It would take eros into itself and begin the long process of learning how human beings through every cell of their bodies might learn to glorify God:

For life, with all it yields of joy and woe,
And hope and fear – believe the aged friend –
Is just our chance o' the prize of learning love,
How love might be, hath been indeed, and is.[15]

John did not go on to describe how love might be between a man and a woman but his gospel shows no trace of fear with regard to sex but a readiness throughout to trust that uncovering process which the Spirit would use to bring human beings to a glad recognition of their mutual self-giving in love. John did not think fit to bring agape into his prologue but reserved a place for it in that declaration of divine intent which he used in reply to the question of Nicodemus. God loved the world so much that he set light and life in it in the person of Jesus Christ that for love's sake the world might be saved. There is nothing here of judgment and condemnation, of punishment and sacrificial atonement but simply a total dependence upon love. He has taken man's flesh born of a woman that the miracle might be wrought in that flesh.

I know of few better descriptions of it than a short essay entitled 'The Nature of Sanctity' written half a century ago by Ida Coudenhove. She took up the somewhat stiff medieval chronicle of the life of Elizabeth of Hungary and made it a vivid testament of love. We know just a little more about this young wife, mother and widow who died at the age of twenty-four than we do about Mary of Magdala or the sisters at Bethany so that we can see something more in her of love incarnate in human flesh. The medium through which we learn something of it is but scaffolding often quite crude but sometimes revealing of great beauty. What we learn of Elizabeth makes one thing clear, that 'the saint in her is only thinkable, is only possible, in the flesh and blood and with the heart and mind of the human Elizabeth'. Though a child in years and virtually powerless in a world of male power, such a woman was able to be, as few men are, unafraid of her human nature. She sought no explanation of love and life but rather their embodiment in bringing them to their true consummation. In the case of Elizabeth and all whom she represents, 'the essence of her humanity is that she is a great lover, a generous heart of incomparable capacity for self-giving'.[16] Hers was the love 'in which passion burns, unmeasured, dangerous'. It is the love that upsets organisation and endures all things, that cherishes the least thing that belongs to the beloved, that goes to the tomb to revere what it loves. A poem of Chinua Achebe on a West African mother-refugee with her dead child, whom 'soon she would have to forget' in her arms, says as much:

> She held
> a ghost smile between her teeth
> and in her eyes the ghost of a mother's
> pride as she combed the rust-coloured
> hair left on his skull and then –
> singing in her eyes – began carefully
> to part it . . . [17]

To do so is to make holy the least fragment of things which pertain to life. I believe that John dreaded the creation of a new priesthood of men to exercise in the Christian communities one more variant form of priesthood that men had set up in the ancient world, as if foreseeing what Blake would one day lament as he looked at the Garden of Love:

And Priests in black gowns were walking their rounds,
And binding with briars my joys and desires

and for that reason gave to women in his gospel as full a measure of the shared ministry of both sexes as he could. It was doomed not to succeed but the seed planted by Jesus of Nazareth did not wither away. Slowly and with many false starts the movement for the emancipation of women from the subjection to which for many centuries they had been condemned made headway as Heloise and her successors found voices to cry out, and poets, novelists and playwrights helped to create a more imaginative perception of womanhood. Without it the agape which is the vitalising theme of the Fourth Gospel must remain simply a word deprived of the flesh and blood that enables it to become an active force in the world. Only a divinised love, an eros set free to become conjugal and able to show men and women how to love instead of dreaming about it could bring mankind and womankind to a true grasp of sexuality redeemed. John intimated that the revelation of its undying presence in the world would be brought to men by the woman. In the words of a poet of our own day, Thomas Blackburn:

Through the intricate metres of their slow advancement
God, through his daughters here, is taking aim.[18]

5

The Johannine Church

What is fatal at present is the superficiality with which the whole *raison d'être* of the Church is treated.

John Bowden, Voices in the Wilderness (1977)

From the beginning, my Church has been what it is today, and will be to the end of time, a scandal to the strong, a disappointment to the weak, the ordeal and consolation of those interior souls who seek in it nothing but Myself.

Georges Bernanos, Bernanos par lui-même

She had never seen the Church as anything other than a centre of drowsiness, an ossified exo-skeleton containing an organism almost inert, pleasantly ruminating sustenance long-champed dry of its vital juices.

Antonia Byatt, The Virgin in the Garden (1981)

May we speak of a Johannine church at all? The word *ekklesia* does not appear in the Fourth Gospel or in the First Epistle of John. In the second epistle bearing his name the 'elect lady and her children' is understood to mean a local church, as is also the elect lady her sister from which the letter was sent. The motherly image of the church caring for her children grew naturally from the deep-seated affectionate reverence for Sion. In the Third Epistle the whole church and a local one experiencing some troubles are clearly referred to.

The word had been known to the Jewish people for a long time. Those who translated their scriptures into Greek had used it. It then meant the congregation of the people of Israel. In the Aramaic usage that possibly lay behind the Greek of

St Matthew's gospel it could have referred to the whole body of them or to a local synagogue's congregation, in much the same way as we speak of a church today.

The absence of the word from the Fourth Gospel is probably not noticed by the majority of its readers, still less by those who only occasionally hear passages read to them during a church service. All take it for granted that it is a biblical word. They recite the creeds which say it is something that Christian people believe in.

There are not lacking among us those who are fervent and enthusiastic about this belief. There are others so often engaged in the difficult tasks of maintaining its presence and work in unfavourable circumstances who are too hard-pressed to welcome much questioning about it. It would hurt them to hear its usefulness queried. They would most probably wince at that kindly dismissive phrase – 'I like going into old churches when I'm on holiday' – used by those who have otherwise written it off. In the rural area in which I live some 80 per cent of people are benignly indifferent to it.

What help the Fourth Gospel can give us in the matter is therefore not easily to be seen. It has nothing to say of an organised ministry or about such matters as baptising babies, marrying couples, burying the dead, maintaining social and charitable organisations, which are to many people today the most familiar aspects of church life. Baptism, marriage and death are referred to in the narrative of the gospel but we learn little from it as to how the earliest Christians dealt with such things. Of devotional practices and relationships with the pagan world it has nothing to say; its austerity in such matters is most clearly evident compared with some second-century writings that made up the apocryphal Acts of John. There the battle for the conversion of pagans has become a fiercely competitive business in which the fanatic, the credulous and the sceptical are all noisily engaged. As for relations with Judaism represented by the Pharisees we learn from other sources that by AD 85 Christian Jews were being expelled from the synagogues. The movement of the disciples of Jesus was being forced to find its way to becoming a church. It was a process that did not lend itself easily to tidy description.

It would be wrong, I believe, to dismiss the matter by saying that the gospel in any case deals with the events of the life and passion of Jesus and ends its narrative almost abruptly soon after mentioning the resurrection. John was writing about what came of those amazing events. His concern was not with what had been but with what was now the light and the life in which he and others rejoiced. The thing that was to be the church had in any case begun its life when Jesus called on some men to follow him.

John's silences are always significant. A reader must be constantly on the lookout for a warning signal. If we have in our minds a notion of a church that apparently is not there, it may well be that that was not the kind of thing John believed Jesus was concerned with. Our picture of the church may be obscuring his. Time after time in this gospel John dwelt on the mistaken reactions of both friends and opponents to what Jesus did and said. It carries the warning that if it could happen then when people were face to face with Jesus, how much more likely it will be that they can get things wrong almost a generation later. Opponents have grown more bitter in their hostility. Believers are tempted to assume that they know how things are or should be.

It was with the latter that John was most concerned. It was for their sake that he wrote the disturbing words: 'After this many of his disciples left him and stopped going with him' (6:66). Open defection was painful but much more important was concealed deviation. In which direction were they really going? In this risky and troublesome business forever involving decisions about how to go forward, on what basis did the Christian communities act? It required of them two things. The first was a resistance to the terrible tendency of men, as Laurens van der Post[1] would one day call it, 'to institutionalise life, building fortresses to hold what they had chosen to select from life'. The second was a willingness to venture 'into the unknown trusting in the guidance of the

Spirit, following Him through the land of Unlikeness, seeking Him in the Kingdom of Anxiety'.

Christians in the last twenty years who have followed the story of the Second Vatican Council have seen these matters highlighted all over again. By our own time the institutional model of the church had so many centuries of acceptance behind it that it had become unthinkable for many to conceive of any other approach. It would sound almost treasonable to suggest that any radical modifications of its structure and ministerial life should be considered. It would seem to many quite absurd to suppose that after nineteen centuries of experience the nature of the church should be in any doubt. To question that now traditional model would be to confuse and foster disunity among the faithful, the very last thing the Holy Spirit could be expected to do. Surely most people must be content to be told by the ministers of the church what to do and what to believe. That this institutional model had for centuries undervalued the ministry of the laity, resisted change as long as it could to the detriment of its own mission throughout the world and even suppressed initiatives on the part of the faithful, was not easily seen or admitted.

The reticence of the fourth evangelist may well have been deliberate. If his gospel was written with some knowledge of what had been happening in the wider field of different Christian communities, he may himself have watched with some misgivings what was taking place. There was much to be glad about and much to question, and always the need to continue to pray for the Spirit's guidance. That there would be diversities of practice and judgment was inevitable. That some men would assume leadership was necessary no doubt but it by no means followed that there was agreement about it. Paul's letters made known the existence of factions within the churches that he had helped to found. In Corinth, it was said, parties claiming to be 'of Cephas, of Apollos, of Paul and even of Christ', had made their appearance. This in a movement whose unity the Lord Jesus Christ had prayed for so earnestly among them! As older members died, as the proportions of Gentile believers to Jews began to change, as new questions of common life and discipline arose, the tensions would be increased. The glad proud expression 'we' would be overtaken by the shadow of 'they', as we see from the First Epistle of John (1 John 2:19). How were they to grow yet remain one body?

Much work has been done by scholars to picture in detail the diversity of growth of the Christian communities during those fateful years. Raymond Brown has for years looked at this matter both from the wide angle and that especially of St John. Writing of the Communities of the Beloved Disciple[2] he had endeavoured to trace the nature of the dissensions which broke out among them, and which he has graphically likened to eaglets tearing at each other with beak and talons disputing for the possesion of the nest. In his book, *The Churches the Apostles Left Behind*,[3] he began his examination of those communities with the question which Browning put starkly in his poem *A Death in the Desert:* 'How will it be when none more saith "I saw"?' He went on to claim that 'most of the New Testament was written after the death of the last known apostle'. A considerable diversity of views about the very nature of the church must have come into being, as indeed the Pauline epistles make clear. How could anyone in the church have doubts about the resurrection, exclaims St Paul, yet it is obvious that there were some who did. Different churches followed various lines of teaching. They would be aware that there would be differences between them. There is a strong sense in the New Testament writings that the unity of the movement must be cherished in spite of such things. The Fourth Gospel is emphatic about the existence of sheep of other folds and the prayer of Jesus that they should all be one flock.

What we have to consider then is whether John saw this not just as a perilous moment when at all costs and by all means they must strive for some kind of unity but as a perfectly natural process of growth in which varieties of insight and breadth of experience contributed to the genuine enrichment of the church as a whole. Did he appreciate a notion of unity which allowed for the maximum degree of freedom to men and women to respond to the Holy Spirit in ways that had not been envisaged before? Did he dread the lack of imagination and charity gaining an upper hand to suppress those manifestations of the Spirit of which some did not approve? Raymond Brown contends that, whatever may have been the case in those far-off days, 'in our present state of a divided Christianity, instead of reading the Bible to assure ourselves that we are right, we would do better to read it to discover where we have not been listening'.

It may well have been so from the earliest days. W. H. C. Frend[4] suggests that this was the case. Far from the mono-lithic body of believers that Gentiles thought it to be or that it was made out to be by some of its adherents, it knew tensions from the outset. Frend comments that 'there never was a time when Jesus' followers were truly united'. He went on to say that 'the difference between "Nazarenes" in Jeru-salem and "Christians" in Antioch as early as c. 39 AD marked the early emergence of an important difference of emphasis between Christians of Palestine and the Dispersion respect-ively.' It may well have accentuated divergences of long-standing character growing up between scattered communi-ties. There was therefore considerable room for the followers of Jesus to develop their own claims to be the true Israel of God. John made his point of view clear in Jesus' words: 'I am the true Vine' (15:1).

A detailed examination of the many sects and parties that arose and flourished at different times during the whole post-Exilic period and throughout the dispersed communities of Jews would make it still clearer that there were any number of precedents for such a movement as that of the followers of Jesus both in Palestine and beyond.

With hindsight we recognise that the great church which emerged in the second and third centuries sought to solve its problems by developing an organised ministry with an increasingly centralised authority, by seeking agreement on certain articles of faith, and by furthering a devotional and liturgical practice that nurtured the inner life of its members. Certain marks of this unified movement were identified. In the creeds they appear to be fourfold. They speak of 'one, holy, catholic and apostolic' church. We may now ask, what part in these things did the Fourth Gospel have. What contribution did it conceivably make to their adoption by subsequent generations?

I turn first to apostolicity. One thing may be remarked on at once. No gospel is so charged with the sense of sending and being sent as that of John yet the word apostle does not appear. Everything of importance in the gospel derives from the statements that 'he whom God hath sent speaks God's words' (3:34), 'there is one who sent me (7:28), 'the Father who sent me is my witness' (8:18), 'I must carry out the work of the one who sent me' (9:4) and many more of like character, leading eventually to the words spoken to the disciples by the risen Christ, 'As my Father sent me, even so send I you' (20:21). How many disciples were present we are not told. Two whose names we are familiar with – Judas and Thomas – were absent. We may remember also that though John does tell us Jesus actually spoke of 'you, the Twelve whom I have chosen' (6:70), throughout his gospel he almost invariably speaks of 'the disciples'. He also gives the impression that they were likely to fluctuate in numbers. When he wrote of the great eucharistic meal he sounds even more strangely vague, 'they were at supper' (13:2).

The contrast with the Synoptic accounts is very marked. From them we learn that at a quite early stage in his ministry Jesus summoned those he wanted and appointed twelve to be his companions, sending them out to preach and to cast out devils (Mark 3:14–16). In St Luke's gospel it is after a night spent in prayer that Jesus selects from his disciples the Twelve 'whom he called apostles' (Luke 3:13). At a later stage these Twelve are sent out to travel from village to village proclaiming the kingdom of God and curing the sick (Luke 9:1–6). A further apostolic mission involving the seventy-two appears later. When the Passover supper is to be eaten Luke tells us that it was with the apostles that Jesus came and in speaking to them during the meal spoke of them as sitting at his table in the kingdom and from their thrones judging the twelve tribes of Israel (Luke 22:30). It was to the apostles that the risen Christ committed the task of witnessing to him. It is when we turn to the Pauline epistles that we hear a new note. The Acts of the Apostles maintain the Lukan references to the Twelve and even describe how the place of the dead Judas was officially filled. Paul however begins his letter to the Galatians by describing himself as an apostle who does not owe his authority to men or his appointment to any human being. He claims to have been so appointed by Jesus Christ and by God the Father. Paul is at pains to insist that what he has preached was the fruit of a revelation made personally to him by the risen Christ and owed nothing to any human being (Gal. 1:11–12). The Christians he now addresses are his children. Though he alludes to the labour of bringing them to birth it is to paternal authority that he turns to require their obedience. There is no court of appeal beyond it. In his first letter to the Corinthians after picturing the mutual dependence of the various members of the body as a true picture of Christian relationships and allowing that each person is a limb or organ of it, Paul abruptly turned it all into a hierarchical system. 'Within our community God has appointed first apostles, secondly prophets, thirdly teachers' (1 Cor. 12:28). He stands to them all in the uncompromising role of an apostle. In his second letter to them he does not hesitate to speak of his critics as 'sham-apostles' and to assert a title to his own authority as based not on any connection with the earthly ministry of Jesus or any authorisation by the Twelve or on his experience of the risen Christ which he alluded to in his earlier letter, but on his mystical experience and his suffering of 'the thorn in the flesh'. It suggests that his sufferings which relate him to those of the Lord are the unassailable credentials of his apostolic authority. Paul was a theological genius but it is difficult to avoid feeling that his recourse to apostolic authority in dealing with the churches smacks as much of political as of religious charisma. He thinks and writes in paternalistic, hierarchical and judgmental terms.

That the Christian churches on the whole came to accept

a pyramidal structure with authority vested in the hands of one man or a few is a matter of history. For some time the lines are a little confused. Apostles, prophets, elders, teachers and bishops and deacons are variously named. In time succession in such offices secured continuity of doctrine and administration. The bishops as heirs of apostolic authority gained general though by no means unquestioned acceptance. Replication of Roman administration went hand in hand with an increasing centralisation. A clerical ministry set apart from the common life of the majority of church members begins to develop its own modes of religious life. Apostolicity was understood to be the keystone of this ecclesiastical structure.

John's reticence about apostles must, I believe, be seen as a questioning of, if not outright opposition to, such a tendency. He went as far as any man could to emphasise the sending of men to continue the work of Jesus. It was their relationship with the whole body of the church which was his concern. Too much was at stake to leave the issues it raised to go unnoticed. The new life and the new way in Jesus would be all too quickly lost to sight if Christians accepted without careful and prayerful concern relationships within the ecclesia that belonged to the very world they were being called upon to renounce. Convinced that Jesus had set before them a very different expression of apostolicity, John was determined to concentrate all attention on that. Whether he had read Paul's letters or not he turned away from the authoritarian tone to a patient attempt to keep the picture of the servant Jesus before his readers. As I have stressed earlier the feet-washing scene must be treated as of cardinal importance. What St Luke chose to put into words of Jesus spoken at that time in the upper room, John turned into drama. 'The kings of the Gentiles exercise lordship over them; and they that exercise authority upon them are called benefactors. But ye shall not be so; he that is greatest among you, let him be as the younger, and he that is chief, as he that doth serve' (Luke 22:25–26). At the very least a new look at all authority, parental, political, rabbinic, priestly, was called for because it was exploited to lay burdens upon human beings instead of fulfilling its true purpose of fostering growth.

Of the servant-Christ I shall try to say more in the following chapter. Here one brief comment upon the scene in the added twenty-first chapter of the Fourth Gospel that bears on this matter may be noticed. It is now not the Pauline but the Petrine authority which would appear to have come under scrutiny. Simon Peter's part in the gospel events is as prominent in this gospel as in the Synoptic accounts. He is mentioned at every important turn in the story. Once again at a meal, though now as the risen Christ, Jesus questions Peter. The searching thrice-repeated 'Simon, son of John, do you love me?' is followed by the emphatic injunction: 'Feed my sheep.' It is to the pastoral service of the shepherd who would lay down his life for the sheep that he is so solemnly committed. If apostolicity was to retain its true significance it could do so only by being lived in the terms which Jesus himself had put to the disciples in the Good Shepherd discourse (10:11–18).

I turn next to holiness, a concept of immemorial antiquity and one most difficult to relate to the modern world. As a dimension of human life it is no longer of general concern. Few people attending church services think of themselves and others present as 'in both seen and unseen worlds' or of those gathered there as the 'holy people of God'. I have heard them called 'the rabble'.

The first thing to notice is how sparing John was with the word 'holy'. It is used only in relation to the Father (17:11) and to the Spirit (1:34 and elsewhere). Whatever holiness attaches to the church depends upon its relation to the Spirit at work. A building set apart for religious practices and an assembly of people meeting there is holy only so far as it is related to or continuous with the divine power at work. The Jewish people along with others shared in the more primitive notions of holiness as an awesome even dangerous power, inexplicable yet demanding of reverence and fear, investing both places and people with special significance yet coming and going as the wind itself. It embraced contraries, light

91

and darkness, silence and speech, stillness and motion. Its root idea when attached to places and people was that of being set apart. Hence the history of the children of Israel was that of a holy people, mysteriously chosen by God and called to live in a covenanted relationship with him.

What distinguished their calling was the ethical nature of it, revealed to the people in Torah. Because he was righteous and merciful, just and loving, Israel's God required of them righteousness, just dealing and love in his people's life. That their history was a chequered one of rebellion and repentance, of falling away and returning, was freely admitted. One feature of Israel's life brought these things to consciousness. The role of the prophets had a unique importance. Through several centuries these holy men bore the word of the Lord God to the nation, themselves summoned and sent by him to recover them to their holy calling. When the voice of prophecy ceased to be heard a perplexed unease became symptomatic of their lost sense of direction.

The point to be made therefore is that the movement that brought into being what was later to be the Christian church began as a groundswell in Israel's life as a holy people. It is unintelligible historically apart from this holy tradition of relationships within and outside the community nurtured through generations. It was as a prophet that men saw John the Baptist and later Jesus the Nazarene. It was as participants in Israel's age-old calling that 'Christians' understood themselves. Such a body does not easily permit an élitism of any kind to break up the totality of its life. 'Would God all the Lord's people were prophets' was a note that expressed an abiding truth which Christian Jews carried with them as their synagogues wrestled with their newest problems. All in all they continued to be a holy people because the Holy Spirit did not forsake them. What they learned from Jesus was a new sense of hope that his holiness was flowering again like Aaron's rod.

Why then the hostility, the complaints and the bitterness leading up to the decision to kill Jesus and threaten a like fate to his friends? I have suggested throughout that John

92

pointed back to what took place when Jesus was going about
his work in order to get his readers to face what was going
on round them and would continue to harass them. It was
his insight into the problems created by changed conditions
that led him to see that every new stage of integration in
life involves and indeed is bespoken by disintegration in the
community's life. As we shall see the end-term of the Johannine vision of what Jesus was about was the one-ness or unity
for which he prayed. It means nothing less than integration
of all human faculties, desires and powers in a process of
living which satisfies personal and social hungers. Men create
religions, empires, arts and sciences to gain measures of integration. Two things beset them with dangers throughout;
their lack of self-knowledge and their changing world. Their
own partial achievements become obstacles to their continued
growth. Turned into idols, religious or secular, they not only
blind their adherents but make them turn fiercely upon
whoever or whatever is felt to challenge their continuance.
The impact crater, as we have called it earlier, is just such a
moment in history when in one man's life a wholly new
principle of integration confronts the society that is far gone
in disintegration. Such was Jewish society when Jesus the
Nazarene came forward and called men and women to a new
way of life. On his head broke the fury of those who chose
suicide rather than a new mode of living.

What this means in terms of the holiness of the Church is
that its members like Isaiah of old know themselves to be in
the presence of God. Embedded in their liturgy is the cry
'Holy, holy, holy', all too easily said or sung, so staggering in
its implications. To pray the Fourth Gospel is to be recovering
something of John's awareness that as the disciples of Jesus
they are led to that presence in and through him. 'The Father
is in me, I am in the Father,' he had said, assuring them that
for that very reason they would continue and even extend his
work. It would be so because the Holy Spirit would come to
and dwell in them (14:26). What John has seen and set out
in dramatic fashion throughout his gospel is that the terrible
radical imperfections of men and women, their blindness,

their selfishness, their self-righteousness, their murderous hatred, cannot defeat this thing which is at work as the result of the coming of Jesus. That is what it means to affirm that the church is holy, a channel of God's grace for the continuing of his work in the world.

As to catholicity or becoming a church universal, what could have been more improbable, more a fantasy of a few dreamers, than that this handful of men and women should think in such terms? Their leader crucified by the Romans, their own nation scornful in its rejection of them, their homeland about to be ravaged by war, how could they suppose that words of that kind applied to them?

Yet that note too is unmistakable throughout the Fourth Gospel. More than any other, though it breathes not a word about Gentiles and talks always with irony or sadness about the Jews, it is addressed to the world. It speaks of the world's salvation with a confidence that is quietly joyful. Its prologue as we saw earlier rejoices because the Light to enlighten mankind has come into the world and the darkness has failed to subdue it. On this narrowest of stages the greatest of all dramatic victories is being played out. The true glory of God has been seen in human flesh by human eyes. The enemy has done all he could and used his last power but the Christ who is risen and ascended has sent the Holy Spirit to continue his work. He will as he promised draw all men to himself.

The foundation of such catholicity lay deep in Israel's history. Its signs were patriarchs and prophets: 'In thee shall all families of the earth be blessed', so ran the Lord God's promise to Abraham (Gen. 12:3). It was repeated to the fugitive Jacob (Gen. 28:14) and to Moses (Deut. 4) as he led a fugitive people. From the root of Jesse there should spring an ensign to the nations (Isa. 11:12) and the Lord God would summon Cyrus, Persia's mighty king, to be his anointed servant for Israel's sake (Isa. 45:4). To Israel the commitment was explicit: 'I will give thee for a light to the Gentiles, that thou mayest be my salvation to the end of the earth' (Isa. 49:6).

The Johannine drama moves vividly to a new point of

revelation with the coming of men called 'the Greeks' desiring to see Jesus (12:20). They are the representative figures of the Gentile world, men seeking to see the world's Saviour. It is one of those moments so characteristic of the Fourth Gospel that points beyond itself to that which may not be seen but which is to be believed. The mission to the world must wait upon the completion of the task Jesus is about the fulfil among his own people through death and resurrection. It must spring from that grain cast into the earth, itself symbol of the dying of Israel to its old life and its being raised to a new one. In the power of the Spirit a new Israel must come into being, a community of peoples in whose relationships a new common life begins to take shape. The God and Father of all mankind sent his Son that the fratricidal wounds of the world's history might be healed, that all nations might come to a peaceful co-existence. The church catholic of the Johannine vision is not one withdrawn from the world but a community in which reconciliation has become the truth incarnate in its manner of living. From the seed thus planted must grow that tree of life 'whose leaves were for the healing of the nations'.

Thus of all the canonical gospels that of John most clearly defines the universal objective of the community that comes into being through Jesus and is activated by the Holy Spirit. It exists to give effect in action to the truth that we are members one of another. One part of its task is to scrutinise the relationships which actually obtain in the societies like nation-states, churches, cities, industrial enterprises, educational institutions and leisure activities, to assess their reality. Do they really express a belonging to one another or an idealised gloss on the situation which masks varying degrees of apartheid? Is the welfare of the weakest members of all those involved the primary concern of the strongest? In calling the one God the Father of all do we seek universal community as the active expression of our faith? At every stage through the first part of John's gospel we are shown how in practice men failed or refused to do what they claimed to believe in. From scrutiny the church must pass to action to repair what is faulty, to supply what is missing, to challenge what obstructs it. Its business like that of its Lord is to give itself as food for the life of God's people without exception.

> How could we be if all were not in all,
> Borne hither on all and carried hence with all,
> We and the world and that unending thought
> Which has elsewhere its end . . . [5]

To say this with the history and present state of the church catholic in mind is to be made painfully aware of the extent to which an idealised form of religion has been substituted for its practice. Belatedly it has begun to examine some aspects of the world it faces, the still hideous subjection of women, the remorseless exploitation of weak underdeveloped peoples, the squalor of the down-town lots of great cities, the blatant differentials of education, racial hatred, anti-Semitism. It has made some gestures of great value in all these fields but with too little overall sense of purpose binding all local congregations together to serve as one body.

It is to the fourth feature, that of unity, we finally come. We face in it as seen from the angle of history, both personal and social, the most sorry examples of failure. In learning to pray the Fourth Gospel it is this which must take priority. In this gospel it is the main theme of the prayer ascribed to Jesus: 'that they may all be one, one in us, as you, Father, art in me and I in You . . . that they may be so completely one that the world will realise that it was you who sent me' (17:21–23). It is first and foremost a unity of personal life which rejects dualist thought that divides body and spirit, the spiritual from the material world, the earthly from the heavenly, the theoretical from the practical. It is secondly a unity of humanity that rejects whatever divides human society and impedes the growth of genuine community on earth.

Perhaps we need first in respect of this twofold task to hear both cries of anguish in the letters of Paul. He has been described as 'the most characteristic of all European figures.' He represents both the strength and the weakness of Europe's life right down to today. We have from him first the admission that personal unity was not his, that he was in the grip of an inescapable dualism. 'What I would, that I do not, but what I hate, that I do . . . so then with the mind I myself serve the law of God; but with the flesh the law of sin'. Paul recognised the conflict in others; 'for the flesh lusteth against the spirit, and the spirit against the flesh; and these are contrary the one to the other, so that ye cannot do the things that ye would'. Release or redemption from this fearful dichotomy came only through death and resurrection, through a divine transaction in which One died for all that through One all might be raised.

At the social level the dualism is no less evident. Having grasped the universal significance of the work of Jesus and stated it clearly: 'there is neither Jew nor Greek, neither bond nor free, neither male nor female', he was overtaken by the realities of estrangement in the world he lived in and fell back upon counselling submission to the conventional social relationships of the day, urging charity but otherwise bowing to them. So for eighteen centuries many Christians would uphold slavery and even fight for its continuance, and for that time too would persecute Jews and deny personal equality to women.

That John saw the church and the work of Jesus in a quite different light seems to me the chief reason for endeavouring to pray the Fourth Gospel. Part of the praying process is learning to look at what Jesus did and what the church now must be doing in the light of Johannine vision. It can only be talked of in terms of 'emerging' but that is now all-important. Much genuine devotion goes to maintaining the churches we have inherited from the past, but so much of what uses up this devotion is trivial and blinkered, spendthrift of resources, insensitive to real problems, diversionary of attention and lacking in imagination. Christians need to know what the Spirit now says to them in their churches and through them to the total life of the world. There are signs of a breakthrough in all parts of the world. The Fourth Gospel can teach us to grow more aware of the winds of the Spirit that are fanning to flame the love of which the Johannine Christ is the divine gesture.

97

6

The Johannine Christ

A great animateur; somebody who breathes life into things.
                    Robertson Davies, *The Rebel Angels* (1982)

One wonders if Christ would have been remembered today if his
divinity had been proclaimed in purely metaphysical terms.
                    Jack Dominian, *Cycles of Affirmation* (1975)

In a real sense the history of christological controversy is the
history of the Church's attempt to come to terms with John's
christology – first to accept it, and then to understand and re-
express it.
                    James Dunn, *Christology in the Making* (1980)

'Through Jesus Christ our Lord.' With such words generations of Christians have prayed to God. They do not excite
surprise any longer. Yet there was a time when they first
began to be used, when a certain breath-taking quality was
attached to them. Paul ended his letter to the Romans saying,
'To God only wise, be glory through Jesus Christ for ever.
Amen.' It was still quite possibly an unusual way of
addressing a prayer to God. How soon it passed into general
use we cannot now say. What we need to do at this point in
our thinking about John's gospel and learning to pray it is to
try to see what an extraordinary leap of thought, feeling and
devotional practice it revealed. How could Jews with their
generations of immediate personal going to God behind them
come to use what sounds like a channelling of prayer through
an intermediary name? What conviction lay behind and
informed this strange unprecedented step?

'We are in union with the Father and with his Son Jesus Christ . . . we have our advocate with the Father, Jesus Christ, who is just.' Already the First Epistle of John suggests that such praying was becoming customary among those Christian communities for whom he wrote. By what steps did they begin to make this devotional journey whose end term is 'in the name of the Father, the Son and the Holy Ghost', embellished and extended with a variety of pious reflections?

We may go back first of all to remind ourselves of Old Testament usage, to what appears to be a stark one to one relation between this man or this people with God in prayer. It is represented in the Fourth Gospel by words ascribed to Jesus, 'I know that thou hearest me always' (11:42). It has the pure immediacy of a relationship that has 'no variableness or shadow of turning'. Reverence dictated reserve in mentioning God's name lest it be profaned or put to wrong use. For the rest, to speak of his name was to mean God himself. 'The name of the God of Jacob defend thee . . . it is a good thing to sing praises unto thy name . . . for thou, Lord, art in the midst of us, and we are called by thy name'. Martin Buber has said[1] that 'god' is the most heavy-laden of all human words. It is possibly the most soiled in use. Yet most people know no better one with which to indicate what is truest in their experience. When they try to say what matters most to them they use this word. Yet it also takes them in a very real sense beyond themselves and then back again to see life afresh. In Buber's words, meeting with God does not come to man in order that he may concern himself with God, but in order that he may realise meaning in the world.

John saw that this was what the disciples had learned from being with Jesus. They gained a new consciousness of God, of him being there in their midst. When he told them at supper to 'trust in God and trust in me' they could feel what that meant. When he promised he would return and take them with him their conviction was simply extended. The words 'I am in the Father and the Father is in me', as astounding a theological utterance as ever a man made, were sober truth. The assurance that 'I will do whatever you ask in my name' and the invitation, 'Ask and you shall receive', were both felt to have a solid foundation in their knowledge of him. When he spoke of sending the advocate Holy Spirit to be with them when he had gone from them, they had wondered what that could mean, very conscious that their minds were being stretched to the very limits of under-standing. Whether their questions were actually voiced at the time hardly matters. Jesus knew they all had such thoughts, that believing in him in those moments was being tested as never before and was being confirmed. Whether they thought of him as the Good Shepherd, as their Master and Friend or as the True Vine, they gained from such imagery enough strength of trust as would survive the darkest and hardest days to come.

It had actually happened. The Fourth Gospel is about human experience. If it led them to make what other men considered outrageous assertions in speaking of him he could only point to what had been put to the test and had been proved true the hard way. John, like others who were now called Christians, was the more convinced by this that they could do no other than address themselves to God 'through Jesus Christ our Lord'. As I emphasised earlier he meant to leave in his readers' minds no doubt whatever about the humanity of Jesus. He himself had seen him tired and angry, seen him weep and rejoice. He had watched him die. He had known what it was to be loved by him. He therefore insisted that he was bone of our bone and flesh of our flesh. But there was also much more to be said about him. Like others he searched round for ways of saying it. He probably knew that Paul called himself 'an apostle of Jesus Christ' and talked of the churches being 'in God our Father and the Lord Jesus Christ' (1 Thess. 1:1). But he himself would not do it lightly. The thing that he sought to say lay in the depths of a personal relation, the I 'in you, you in me,' the meaning of which only the years of life in the world could evaluate.

In the meantime many questions had to be faced. What did it really mean to speak of Jesus as the Christ and Lord? What relationship with God the Father was implied by that

100

'and' which coupled his name with that of Jesus? How meaningful was the title Christ in the Gentile world? We who read this gospel today might well ask what it says to us. The modern use of Christ the King has revived what was at the heart of an ancient usage.

The Messianic title had been in use among Jews for centuries. It would have become known to those Gentiles interested in Judaism. Its significance in Jewish history was varied. It referred both to those styled Messiah in the past and to expectations about the future. From time to time it was applied to some contemporary leader. From the Dead Sea Scrolls we can learn of a prophet-Messiah, a priest-king Messiah, a revealed, concealed or a slain Messiah. The mainstream use was of a kingly Messiah of the house of David. On him were set the hopes of generations for a saviour who would overwhelm the heathen, restore Israel's kingdom to full power, rebuild Jerusalem and make its temple the spiritual centre of mankind. For some a more mystical idea prevailed. The coming of Messiah would inaugurate an age of righteousness, purity and peace. To the Pharisees it represented both a political and spiritual ideal. All in all it was a root-stock so deeply implanted in Jewish hearts that it outlived all disappointments and defeats. In the latter half of the seventeenth century it could send up the strange shoot of Sabbatai Sevi and his prophet Nathan of Gaza to draw many thousands of Levantine Jews to a new hope of Messianic fulfilment.

As a title therefore it was neither blasphemous nor offensive. It was the guileless Nathanael who at his first meeting with Jesus hailed him as the king of the Jews. It did however alarm the Sadducees, the priestly clan ruling the temple, and the Herodian faction. Both were anxious to collaborate with the Romans and to avoid any further punitive measures which might be taken to quell political unrest. The appearances of Jesus in Jerusalem to which the Fourth Gospel gives great prominence alarmed them. The Palm Sunday episode may well have been the last straw that broke their patience. The more pious Jews would have had no such feelings. They would have felt no great desire to defend the building which Herod had built. On the other hand they had heard strange things about Jesus of Nazareth being ready to consort with people of very dubious character.

The title Messiah meant simply being anointed. It signified to the person concerned and to the world that this person was appointed to and invested with the dignity and powers of an office like that of king. Such symbolic acts were, as Mary Douglas has pointed out,[2] socially determined and most frequently referred to the body, as in ceremonies of the laying-on of hands, dressing in particular garments, crowning, anointing and seating upon a throne the person chosen. The British coronation ceremonial has preserved much of this traditional behaviour, relating this person to God. 'Thou hast loved righteousness and hated iniquity; therefore God hath anointed thee with the oil of gladness above thy fellows.' Quite understandably Shakespeare's Richard II refused to believe that such balm could ever be washed away. Charles I died believing it still to be so. Yet Samuel's cautious secrecy at the first anointing of David left little doubt that it could always involve political danger.

Given the social conditions of Galilee and Judaea at the time when Jesus came forward, Messianic hopes could not but have been excited. Social symbols at times of stress take on added power, as the Nazis would one day demonstrate to Europe. In his study of millennialism in medieval times Norman Cohn has described how the areas which saw the rise of mass hysteria and popular crusades were those which had been repeatedly swept by famine, drought and plague for many years.[3] Starving labourers, beggars and orphaned children together with frightened gentry and uneasy nobles rushed out to take the Holy Land from the Turks. As an alternative they could massacre the Jews. Where the home-land had borne the burden of alien and heathen rule reaction could never be other than violent. Pompey's capture of Jerusalem in 63 BC marked a turning point in Jewish history. It furthered the outflow of the dispersion of Jews. It stoked the fires of insurrection at home. Such was one powerful aspect of Messianism when Jesus appeared.

One feature of the four gospels has now to be noted. Though questions most naturally arose as to whether he could be Messiah, he himself said little about it and seems to have discouraged both his disciples and the crowds from speaking openly of it. John makes it clear that while he could not avoid all such references to himself his mind as regards his work lay elsewhere. He must have realised very quickly that he could not avoid being put to death by the Romans by being crucified, but he had in the meantime to show his disciples what was worth dying for even if the alleged reasons for taking his life were quite false. The extent to which John the evangelist saw this is made clear in his account of the confrontation of Jesus and Pilate.

The situation was changed by the death and resurrection of Jesus but it was still a matter of different views. Paul and Luke were quick to proclaim the crucified Messiah, announcing that 'God hath made this crucified Jesus both Lord and Christ'. How many of Jesus' disciples made that theological leap it is hard to imagine. It could not have been anything but blasphemous to most Jews and certainly to strict pietists to use the name *kurios* or Lord in its divine sense of a human being who had recently lived among them and had suffered the degradation of death on the cross. To speak of 'being in Christ' furthermore could sound very near to embracing the language of various mystery cults which were common enough at the time.

In the case of *kurios*/Lord we are, as Geza Vermes has shown, in a veritable minefield of terminology. He points out the innumerable respectful uses of the word common in the society of the day, such as find their way into the Fourth Gospel from the lips of the court official who asked for Jesus' help for his sick child, from the crowd in the story of Lazarus, from Peter in the feet-washing scene and elsewhere, from Mary of Magdala speaking to the supposed gardener and to the two disciples as she tells them of the empty tomb. All this against a background of usages in the Hellenistic world that had many connotations of divinity.

What we face in reading how these various titles were used to speak of Jesus is not only the old difficulty of making old words say something new but also the changing of people's ideas in situations of stress and tension. There are few if any terms on which everyone agrees or which continue over any length of time to retain their original or earlier meanings. The writer of Acts said that the earliest preaching of the apostles in Jerusalem was that 'God had made this Jesus both Lord and Christ', that is to say long before the gospels came to be written. In certain Pauline epistles which in all probability also preceded the gospels the grace of God and the Lord Jesus Christ is the common form of salutation. 'May God our Father and the Lord Jesus Christ send you grace and peace.'

When we turn to the gospels it appears that customary usage applied the word lord to miracle-workers, as several examples in St Matthew's gospel make clear. In St Luke, who calls Jesus Lord a great many times, a much wider range of meanings including those of teacher, prophet and Messiah, are apparent. John's use, as we have just seen, is equally varied but moves to a tremendous climax in the final scene of what was presumably the conclusion of the gospel as originally planned. There Thomas acknowledges his Master with the words: 'My Lord and my God.' Taken together with the author's statement that his purpose was to help readers to believe that Jesus was indeed the Christ, the Son of God, it could well be said that this was 'the most advanced interpretation of the Messiahship of Jesus'. The question remains however whether this did mark an irrevocable break with strict Jewish monotheistic thought. I note Hyam Maccoby's dismissal of the Fourth Gospel as the 'latest and least authentic of the Gospels' and as 'lacking all the Jewish flavouring found in the other Gospels' which do identify Jesus as a Jewish teacher.[4]

Did it happen like that? I have no Jewish scholarship with which to contend with Maccoby's judgment. I must freely admit that some time while John was writing or being read the break with what was to be the Judaism of the future took place. The first seeds of an evil anti-Semitism were being sown and John's use of the words 'the Jews' to describe the opponents of Jesus was to do an immense amount of harm. With that awful legacy culminating in the holocaust it is difficult to do more than silently acknowledge before all else our terrible common Christian culpability. How can we pray to the God and Father of all mankind unless we do so? How dare we hail Galilean Jesus as Lord and turn away from his people?

While there is time we must do what we can. As mortal and fallible human beings we must not treat human works as absolutes. The New Testament, written indeed by men inspired by the Holy Spirit, is neither historically nor theologically an absolute set beyond human limitations, any more than our subsequent interpretations of it can claim to be. There is none good in the absolute sense but God. The Conciliar Statement known as *Nostra Aetate*, issued in October 1965, began to try to undo some of the hideously wrong things said and done to Jews since the first century. It has been both welcomed as a step forward and much criticised for its great failings. Perhaps the best that can be said is to welcome the fact that the dialogue has begun. I believe it is possible furthermore to read the Fourth Gospel as the work of a man who was more than most men of that time aware of the impact crater occasioned by Jesus and the problems it raised for everyone close enough to it to feel the disturbance it created. He was no Paul quick to interpret Jesus in a theological synthesis that could be preached to both Jews and Gentiles with a dazzling display of authority and an eloquence that appeared to meet every need. He was nevertheless an equally gifted man who chose to follow his own line of interpreting Jesus to his fellow disciples, steering clear as far as he could from too hasty a formulation of the theological significance of the One who loved him and a too hasty attempt to institutionalise the life of the community which had grown out of Jesus' work. He wanted rather to wait on the Spirit at work among them.

John believed in the transcendent, in the self-transcendence which is, in Viktor Frankl's words, the essence of existence.[5] He wanted to make room in his gospel for human imagination to be free and fearless enough to transcend all those titles of Messianism that men were accustomed to using. He sought to awaken them to spiritual response such as no one as yet had discerned. His own task as a poet was not just to make the words that were familiar mean more than most people had ever guessed but to call on his fellow-Christians to make the imaginative leap that loving inspires. He would have understood what William Blake would one day say about his own version of the 'Everlasting Gospel':

> I'm sure this Jesus will not do
> Either for Englishman or Jew.

He remembered the difficulties that so many people had voiced: could Messiah be like this? Do the authorities believe him to be Messiah? Could a Galilean be the Messiah? He could not have stopped them from asking such questions but he wanted to lift them right out of that kind of thinking and to focus their eyes anew on Jesus. 'This is life eternal, to know you, the only God, and Jesus Christ whom you have sent.' John knew that the sending never stopped; so neither could the learning to know him.

It must go on now. We must be continually asking, what is Jesus Christ for us today? When Graham Sutherland was asked to design the great tapestry for the new post-war cathedral in Coventry he discussed at some length with others concerned with the project the representational imagery he wanted to use.[6] We may see from his sketchbooks how widely his imagination roved. He set aside very many conceptions of the Christ figure as too hackneyed. He wanted, he said, to relate his figure to the contemporary world, a thing which artists had of course been doing since they first began to depict the Christ at all. In many famous mosaics the Lord appears attired much as a well-dressed Roman emperor might

have looked. But Sutherland meant more than that. He felt
'the need for a tragic and sombre element' because he had
lived through the epoch of Buchenwald and Auschwitz,
through times of worldwide violence and unparalleled
destruction. On the other hand he sought to present 'a figure
of great contained vitality', one that had 'in its lineaments
something of the power of lightning and thunder, of rocks, of
the mystery of creation generally – a being who could have
caused these things, not only a specially wise human figure'.
It was very much a Johannine Christ – the creative Logos,
the Son of Man, the majesty of God's Son – that he spoke of.

Sutherland's tapestry should send us back to the poem that
has supplied the title for this book. Since painting does not
find a place in it I would add Chaim Potok's novel, *My Name
is Asher Lev*,[7] to supply a further comment upon what is being
attempted through all the material resources of words, stone,
paint, sound, as means to revelation and concealment of God.
It may well be true that 'painting is not for Jews', that its
values are 'goyisch and pagan', but Potok's novel about
painting says more clearly than most books I have read what
every kind of artist faces and attempts to do. John the evangelist is among them working with words. He, along with
them all, is tooling the events of his story that his Christ-
figure may be to us his readers what John claims him to be,
the truth of life itself.

Two things may be said about the task that must have a
place in our prayer reading of it. The first concerns the human
limitations of every such work. The sculptor Naum Babor
said that 'every work of art is by its nature incomplete, that
is, only half-created, until it has been finished by the
beholder'. The work, in other words, is a shared experience.
The artist or writer can evoke our response but we ourselves
must be giving to it to enable it to fulfil its author's intention.
If in such matters 'we receive but what we give', how do we
become givers? If we are to learn what Christ is for us today
must it not require finding those who make up the 'us'? Can
those who are alienated from each other give to the common
stock of shared understanding?

The second thing concerns what comes down to us as the traditional or customary way of viewing the artist's work. A long-settled habit of mind about it may in fact be stifling any lively response. Both pietism and narrow fanaticism can exclude the full breadth of life which is the necessary ground for any true appreciation of such work. That does not entirely preclude a breakthrough from time to time when men rediscover the things that have been for so long hidden away and neglected. It can mean none the less a steady impoverishment of consciousness so that 'from him that hath not even that which he hath shall be taken away'.

Both these affected the way in which John's gospel and his presentation of Christ were read and evaluated at the time of writing and in subsequent years. To his own generation, to secure the fullest co-operative response, he appealed by making use of the great themes of Messiah and Logos, Son of God and Son of Man, interwoven dramatically with the events of the life, death and resurrection of Jesus. He did what every poet and artist must do to be read at all, while keeping open his own line along which he is free to say what is his uniquely personal thing. Where a man fails to hold these in balance he becomes either prisoner to current understanding and taste or largely unintelligible and therefore neglected. Blake's poetry is an example of the latter while the names of those who were once merely best-sellers are quickly forgotten. The Fourth Gospel pursued its own line so markedly that it became both an object of some suspicion to the more orthodox-minded yet a fertile source-book to those who felt the need to develop a more adequate theological expression of Christian life and belief. John would seem to have pondered deeply upon the words he ascribed to the risen Christ speaking to Mary Magdalene: 'Don't try to hold me, but go to the brothers and tell them that I am ascending to my Father and your Father, to my God and your God.' He sought therefore to allow for further growth in understanding of the significance of the Christ. His gospel did in fact come to influence very profoundly the christological controversies of subsequent years.

108

Even so there was a high price to be paid for being so influential. No poet can control what men will make of his work in years to come, though in so far as he touched the deepest levels of human experience later generations will return to him. The eighteenth-century fashion of rewriting Shakespeare's plays and giving King Lear a happy ending eventually yields to rediscovery of the more challenging and significant work of the original author. John's fate was to be both much used, perhaps even misused, and neglected. One thing however stands out. His words with regard to the incarnate Lord, 'of his fulness have we all received' (1:16), were to be proved true in almost every direction of thought and devotional practice in Christian experience from the first century onwards. The multiplicity of the imagery with which Jesus of Nazareth has been presented to the world through nineteen centuries has been due in no small measure to the range of John's vision.

Turning first to the theological field and to that aspect which gives title to James Dunn's book, *Christology in the Making*,[8] we find this scholar describing the Fourth Gospel as 'the climax of the evolving thought of first-century Christian understanding of Christ'. He was not so much the inventive author of great concepts like the Wisdom-Logos or the divine Sonship as the imaginative craftsman who found a way of weaving them together. He applied himself to the task because he was sensitive to the age-old need on the one hand of giving to the Jewish conception of God a personal relationship with human beings and on the other of enabling the Gentile world to grasp the cosmic significance of Jesus Christ. 'He identified the impersonal Logos with the personal Son, and presented Jesus as the incarnate Logos who explains the unseeable God.' He made an imaginative leap 'from thinking of Jesus as the content of the word of preaching to identify him as the divine Logos become incarnate'. He did so not with theologians in mind but for the sake of the friends of Jesus, of whom he was one, who were daily contending for such a faith. First and last his purpose is a pastoral one just as our prayer reading of his gospel should be. It was a pastoral concern that would embrace all sorts and conditions of men and women in all ages, whether mystics like Catherine of Genoa or novelists like Tolstoy.

But the range of influence of the Johannine Christ was to be immense. It was not simply in the imagery which came into being to portray the many aspects of his nature but in the lines of thought and behaviour which were so strongly inspired by the gospel itself that the indebtedness of the whole world to John was revealed. Thus Jaroslav Pelikan in surveying the place of Jesus in the history of culture, that is to say the life of society including its arts, philosophy, politics, and social affairs, can begin with John's triad of Jesus as the Way, the Truth and the Life (14:6) as corresponding to, though not identical with, the classical triad of the Good, the True and the Beautiful.[9] He will conclude with the Man who belongs to the world who in the Fourth Gospel speaks of himself as its light and the world as the object of his love. He asks whether anti-Semitism would have grown to such evil proportions if Christians had kept in mind Jesus' warning to his friends: 'the hour is coming when whoever kills you will think that he is offering service to God' (16:2). He suggests that the cosmos could be treated as 'reliably knowable and at the same time infinitely mysterious as the concept of Logos passed into human thought in Western Europe to portray the Mind and Reason of God'.

It is not only in such seminal conceptualisations that this influence is to be studied. The great bulk of the Fourth Gospel is taken up with a description of personal relations. It could be said to begin with Jesus inviting some men to stay with him and learn from that personal contact what manner of man he was. From then on they were given the opportunity to watch and listen to him as he faced the critics of what he was doing. It was evident that he crossed social barriers, that he was deeply concerned with the marginalised people of society, that he saw no reason why current styles of behaviour should not be challenged, and that while he was prudent he was also fearless.

John realised quickly that this manner of living was what

Jesus meant by loving. He saw in it the explanation of Jesus' teaching that men must learn to love one another. He heard it related to God when Jesus claimed to be doing both what God himself did and what he had sent his Son also to do. It put all religious practice upon a new basis. Believing in God was not subscribing to what men said of him but responding to what God required of those he confronted. To become alive to a world understood in that way was to gain a wholly new vision of it. One had to decide to be for or against it on the basis of trusting this Jesus.

John was clearly anxious that it should be understood as loving. At first sight it would have appeared to have very little to do with what most people thought of as loving, so completely had sexual relationships come to engross their thinking. They had learnt all too little from the earliest relationship of life to illuminate its further stages. The aspects of mutuality, dependence, freedom, of giving and receiving, got lost to sight and the chances of learning from others were being missed. Loving, as Viktor Frankl has described it in our day, as 'living the experience of another person in all his uniqueness and singularity', stood little chance of being valued as such. Society was for the most part content to accept the drive of sexuality to be for most people the nature of love. It had the strength of consumerism to sustain it. The love of the sexes finds little place in the gospels. Hasty judgment might well infer that the Johannine Christ had little to do with this vast area of human experience, yet of all the gospels that of John dwells more deeply upon the nature of loving than any other. It bases everything upon the Godhead who is Love. It makes clear that the relationship of God with mankind is the expression of love and the renunciation of that of power. In this way that God loves the world, men and women in turn are invited to learn through every stage of their creaturely existence what it means to be loved and loving. He made himself one with us that by that union we might learn to know him. The kingdom of God was itself God revealing himself to his people that they might find fulfilment of their nature in him.

111

Our attempt to pray this gospel must however mean more than contemplating the wealth of description and implication that is brought to the Christ in its pages and that it caused to grow in subsequent centuries. Pelikan's book, rich as it is, does but begin to indicate the directions in which this Christ-figure may be found to have inspired men and women of every kind. Nor can we leave out of the picture the part that John's Christ was to play in the great theological battles during which the Christian church put together its creeds. 'What think ye of Christ?' will go on setting fresh reflection in motion no doubt for years to come. The final outcome in terms of artistic response is not to be found in Holman Hunt's *Light of the World* or the Sacred Heart or in Dali or Chagall. Potok's novel helps to say why:

> For the Master of the Universe, whose suffering world I do not comprehend, for dreams of death, for the love I have for you, for all the things I remember, and for all the things I should remember but have forgotten, for all these I created this painting – an observant Jew working on a crucifixion because there was no aesthetic mould in his own religious tradition into which he could pour a painting of ultimate anguish.[10]

Was that the picture John intended to leave in the minds of his readers? I quoted earlier Graham Sutherland's ruminations on what he wanted to do in the Coventry tapestry. John did after all put down in words what he sought to do. Can we begin to pray our own discernment of the essential feature of his Christ?

I believe we shall find it given dramatically and laconically in a very few words: '*Ide ó ánthropos, ecce homo,*' 'Look, here is Man'. In the Gospel as a whole the meaning is filled out in terms of the experience that John and others had had. Here is the man who had drawn them to himself, who had loved them and taught them the meaning of love. Here was the man crucified by the demonic evil powers of the world, but the man who had quite simply conquered it by giving his whole life for the sake of the world's lost children. Here was the man who had broken through all the barriers that divided men and women from each other and built up between them distrust and fear. Here was the man who had shown equal understanding of men and women, who had shown both grief and hope in the way through suffering and death, who had taught them the meaning of trust in the simplest channels of everyday life.

But something more had yet to be said of this man, the hardest and strangest thing that, but for all that had gone before and had taken place since, it would have been almost impossible to speak rightly. This man had died. Some of his friends had had moments thereafter when he appeared to be among them confirming his words that they would see him again, confirming the promise that he would give them the Holy Spirit. But, and here I think John is quietly adamant, this was not what the Johannine Christ must be thought to be, however moving the experience to those who claimed to have seen him. To a woman, Mary of Magdala, to a man, Thomas, one of the Twelve, the word is the same: 'don't cling to the vision to make a glory of thy silent pining'. What matters is the trust in God that he begot in you, the trust through which you will have access to God for every moment of your life. Personal life is finite but every moment of it can become significant of eternal life and incandescent with glory. That was how the Johannine Christ had lived among them. That was what he had promised they would come to know 'through him' and by his being 'amongst them'. What he had been was closed in human terms as a thing of the past, what he was in human hearts and minds they were now and henceforward for ever committed to learn through the Holy Spirit who would be with them and in them. Because he the Johannine Christ had been, they were new men and women.

7

The Johannine Spirit

The Holy Spirit is totally primordial.
John Taylor, *The Go-Between God* (1972)

Theology pays too little attention, on the whole, to the immanence of God in Man.
Geoffrey Lampe, *God as Spirit* (1983)

In the present order of things, Divine Providence is leading us to a new order of human relations.
John XXIII, Second Vatican Council

To pray the Fourth Gospel means above all other things to pray in and for the guidance of the Holy Spirit. It means praying with a concern as wide as life itself. The Holy Spirit was confessed to be Lord and giver of life in the Nicene Creed. The task set to the Christian church was then, now and as it was at its beginning, to learn what believing in such a Spirit does mean in terms of living.

This gospel was written to help in that process of learning, to throw as much light as possible on the venture of faithful living to which John and his readers were committed. It was a reminder not just of the circumstances in which that way of life had been taken on but of how the Holy Spirit came into it and was still at work in it. It reminded them that the beginning lay not in themselves but in God. It was a gospel of course because it brought glad tidings for what in their hearts they had yearned for. It called to them and they had answered. The important thing nevertheless was that the call had come to them from him, the God in whom they had

114

trusted and through Jesus Christ whom they believed he had sent. They were not a group of like-minded people who had met and agreed to experiment with a new mode of living but disciples of a man who had called them to follow him, to learn from him how the life he was set upon could be lived.

They were still learning now, years later, though he had gone to the death that he had told them would come. The learning process had had to go on with the help of the Holy Spirit. That help Jesus had promised them also. They would find out for themselves, he had said, that they could do the things they had learnt from him and even do more. This too had proved to be true. So when John writes of the things that took place in those years long past when Jesus had worked among them, it is not their pastness that concerns him but the illumination they give to what the Holy Spirit is teaching them now.

I believe this is the most important thing that we have to learn from John's gospel. Of course we have to study the text to see and understand how this venture of faith began, but our purpose is not to end up with a doctrine of Holy Spirit but to be more aware of that Spirit at work now. It was with that in mind that Pope John XXIII summoned the Second Vatican Council, to which he and his successor devoted several encyclical letters. What has long been needed by the whole Christian church is an extended confession of faith in the workings of the Holy Spirit. It was right to acknowledge the life-giving Godly power 'proceeding' as the true object of Christian worship. It was good to mention the prophets through whom the Spirit had spoken. But what the Christian church needs is a much more explicit and fuller assertion of what these prophets have said and who they are. Prophets still for most people are biblical characters or those with some insights into the future. They do not see them as men and women who search for the truth in every human situation and tell us what it looks like no matter how unpopular or demanding it is. They do not expect the Holy Spirit to be as disturbing as this. What enthusiasm for the Spirit there is tends to express itself in acts of personal piety and charitable concerns. All too rarely does it recognise the confrontation of ways of life in the world in which it becomes necessary to take sides.

It was for this reason that John shaped his gospel as a disclosure of what the continuing action of the Holy Spirit would be like. It was why he took such liberties in the arrangement and presentation of his story.

Consider briefly the people for whom he was writing. It was not what we call today a mass movement. The only instance of that in this gospel is the crowd that wanted to make Jesus their king and from which he walked away. John's readers were probably few in number. Their neighbours were mostly indifferent or hostile to them. They were all living in a time of social upheaval. The Christians though a minority group were not easily defined to themselves or to others. Though they shared in and greatly prized something which came to be called *koinonia*, a sense of community in which they experienced love, joy and peace, long suffering, kindness and goodness, they were really engaged in discovering how this new life should grow in freedom from fear and towards still more wholesome life.

As Jews they had scriptures, long tradition, symbols and rites, which they valued greatly but which Jesus had taught them to regard in a changed way. They were learning that God the Spirit was to be worshipped, in and through, not holy places nor traditional offerings but the life of the holy community and the relationships within and outside it. As regards their traditional religious equipment they were finding out by the hard test of experience what was helpful and what they no longer could use. They sang the old songs of Sion but found themselves giving new content to them. They longed for peace and security but it had to be his peace and the kind of trust in God that they had seen in him.

It was then for a people spiritually, behaviourally and mentally on the move that John wrote his gospel. If his prologue had roots in Genesis, his narrative took up the theme of the Exodus. They were albeit in changed circumstances on the march once again to what had been variously called the

Promised Land, the Holy City, the kingdom of God and
eternal life. They could be reminded of that presence that
had gone up with Moses, that had been pictured as a pillar
of cloud by day and a fiery column at night, and no less
powerfully as a still small voice. Now it was the presence of
that advocate Spirit which Jesus had promised would be with
them to guide them into all truth. That meant truth in living.

We can know but little of their experience of it in the
whole round of daily life. What has come down to us are the
evidences of their devotional practice in such things as the
laying-on of hands, prophesying and speaking with tongues,
fragments of liturgy and lections that kept before people's
minds how the Spirit had come and worked among them.
'Established custom', wrote Dr Johnson after touring in Scot-
land and thinking back to the Union, 'is not easily broken,
till some great event shakes the whole system of things, and
life seems to recommence upon new principles.' Pentecost in
the account in Acts was plainly to the writer such an event
but by no means the only aspect to be remembered of the
working of the Holy Spirit. More significant perhaps was the
later occasion when after the release of Peter and John by the
Sanhedrin the Christian community in Jerusalem met and
prayed for help. 'As they prayed, the house where they were
assembled rocked, they were all filled with the Holy Spirit
and began to proclaim the word of God boldly' (Acts 4:31).
There followed a great gesture of sharing in common all that
they possessed.

However much John knew of the writings of the other
evangelists and Paul about the Holy Spirit he was clearly
determined to go his own way in presenting the matter to his
readers. It was from the vantage-point of deeply considered
belief both in what Jesus had said of the Spirit and what his
own reflection and experience had taught him that he went
to work. He had become convinced that the words spoken by
Jesus were as he himself had said 'Spirit and life'. They were
the very essence of the new life, itself a kind of new creation.
Life however is not something given once for all and

117

completed but something that is lived and known only in day to day living:

> So duly, daily, needs provision be
> For keeping the soul's prowess possible,
> Building new barriers as the old decay,
> Saving us from evasion of life's proof,
> Putting the question ever, 'Does God love,
> And will ye hold that truth against the world?'[1]

The new life expressed itself in loving. It was the presence of the Holy Spirit that made loving possible and actual. So John made his book culminate in one scene in which Jesus breathed into men the spirit or breath of this new life. I have long felt that John omitted from his account of what took place in the room at supper the words, 'Do this in remembrance of me', not because he did not value them as he did every word that Jesus had ever spoken, but because the more important thing lay in the gift of the Spirit. Nothing must be allowed to divert attention from this. The holy meal, the fellowship, the feasting on every word that proceeded out of God's love, were inestimably precious, but their reality for men and women depended upon the presence and active power of the Spirit. How could they pray unless the Spirit inspired them? Had Jesus not warned them that the flesh profited nothing even though he had talked of giving his own flesh and blood as their food? Not even his words repeated in days to come could be life-kindling if detached from the Spirit.

The working foundation of the new movement was therefore to be stated as clearly as possible. It is in fact repeated many times in the account of what was said at the supper. 'I shall ask the Father and he will give you another Advocate to be with you for ever, that Spirit of truth whom the world can never receive' (14:16–17); 'When the Advocate comes whom I will send to you from the Father, the Spirit of truth who issues from the Father, he will be my witness' (15:26); 'Unless I go, the Advocate will not come to you, but if I do go I will send him to you' (16:7); 'But when the Spirit of truth comes, he will lead you to the complete truth, since he will not be speaking as from himself, but will say only what he has learnt' (16:13).

So important was this that John did even more than repeat such words. He did what no other evangelist did with the basic story. He treated the death, resurrection and ascension of Jesus as nearly as possible as one event. He made it the condition of the Spirit's coming, and that outpouring of Spirit the consummation of everything that had had its place in the story. Not a word here about giving his life a ransom for many or atonement, mediation or sacrifice but simply that this is the way by which the Holy Spirit has been given. 'The Spirit comes', to quote Geoffrey Lampe's words, 'as the new mode of Christ's presence, made possible by the death through which the life of Jesus takes on a new dimension.'[2] The Christian calendar has marked out the years since the birth of Christ. A much more truly Johannine use would have reminded us that we have lived since that day when Mary of Magdala went to the tomb at first light and on whose evening the disciples assembled to receive their commission in the Age of the Spirit.

We have now to consider how this momentous declaration could have been understood at that time and how it stands with us today. Although there is reference to a future coming of Jesus in the appended Chapter 21, John's gospel virtually divided human history into two parts, the time when God spoke to mankind through intermediaries like angels or prophets or in dreams, and the time in which he now speaks to human hearts and minds through his own presence to them. How far, we may ask, had Jewish thinking moved towards this latter? What meaning does it have for us in the twentieth century?

The lengthy reflection upon the Spirit in the Old Testament embraced both the creation and sustaining of all things by divine power and those relations between God and man which were to become the hallmark of Israel's history. A degree of polarisation is always observable. At one end the distinction between man and his maker is absolute. God is in heaven, his ways are not ours, and man's life is but a stirring of dust.

At the other God talks with his creature in friendly fashion, makes known to him what he purposes for mankind, enters into a covenant with him and will go to all lengths to hold him to it. In his fatherly care he sends leaders and judges, kings and prophets to maintain a relationship befitting the children of such a God. Because he is righteous he will require righteousness of life among men. Conversely because men set their love upon him he will keep them in all their ways. 'With long life will I satisfy him: and show him my salvation.' It left scope for the poetic imagination of the author of Job to postulate a human integrity which transcended even those terms.

What was most significant in that relationship of the spirit was the dialogue into which men were drawn. Prophets as mere human mouthpieces of the Lord might rightly bewail their tainted lips but the Lord himself would see to their purging. Ezekiel, quite properly, would fall on his face on being addressed by the Lord in his glory but that same Lord required him to stand on his feet to hear his apostolic commission. Since the Lord God was no respecter of man-made honours he chose whom he would for such awesome tasks, and sent them to tell their news whether or not those they spoke to would listen. The cost of so doing might well be derision or death.

All this should be seen as the most fitting preparation for the gospel drama. Though the line of great prophets had mysteriously ended with Malachi no more emphatic charge and promise could have been made than his, with that promise to send Elijah 'before the coming of the day of the lord'. The fierce anger of Joel was none the less coupled with that most gracious of all the Lord's words:

I will pour out my spirit upon all mankind,
Your sons and your daughters shall prophesy,
your old men shall dream dreams,
and your young men see visions,
Even on slaves, men and women,
Will I pour out my spirit in those days. (Joel 3:28–29)

120

So the great Jewish tradition of revelation prepared the way for that outright direction of all attention upon the presence of the Spirit which was to be the Johannine gospel. It came as a power from without (for men are not God) but, in Buber's words, 'not in such a way as to make of man a vessel to be filled or a mere mouthpiece, but to take possession of the existent human element and recast it . . . revelation is encounter's pure form'.[3]

The endowment of Jesus of Nazareth with the Holy Spirit is common witness in all the canonical gospels. All related it to the time of his baptism at the hands of John the Baptist. All described it in symbolical fashion with the descent of the dove. John alone added the Baptist's testimony to 'the Lamb of God that takes away the sin of the world' (1:29). Much scholastic commentary has been devoted to this enigmatic utterance for which the evangelist offered no explanation, but the reference to the world needs to be noted. Something designed to reach out to the ends of the world is in motion. The first breath of the wind that is the Holy Spirit has touched a human forehead in Bethany beyond Jordan. In such symbolic terms a new age in human history is being announced. Even more apt for the occasion perhaps is reference to the river, the great underground river to which one day Meister Eckhart would turn men's attention as being a true symbol of God's creativity, 'the river that no one can dam up and no one can stop'.[4] To be born of that water and the Spirit is to be alive to the coming of God's kingdom.

The references to the kingdom of God in the Fourth Gospel and teaching about its nature are few compared with those set out in the Synoptists' work. They are nevertheless important and placed at decisive points in the presentation of Jesus' work. There is nothing 'other-worldly' about it though it is not the product of human ambition and contriving. It is 'my kingdom', says Jesus as he stands before Pilate. 'It can only be entered through a spiritual rebirth', says Jesus to Nicodemus. In both cases the men well-placed in a worldly sense are puzzled and unable to grasp what he means. They are quite unprepared to see that Jesus was talking about a relationship between God and man which is the basic truth of the latter's existence. That relationship is being made explicit to men and women in and through Jesus Christ. His very presence is the witness to and evidence of God's love for his people and his will that they should have eternal life, that is to say, enter the kingdom. The Spirit is not only the energy of God's life-giving purpose but the light that enlightens all those who are vitalised by it.

We too stand in danger of missing the truth of this exactly like Nicodemus and Pilate as long as we fail to rise to the demand which Jesus calls 'being born through the Spirit'. Put in other words it means failure to accept the conditions of integrity of life and thought that pertain to our human condition. The world and mankind are the outcome of the Spirit's creative act. It is the business of man to discern this truth of his nature and place in the whole order thus brought into being. His job is learning the truth through a quite fearless identification of himself with the bringing to birth process. Hence Jesus very steadily calls on men and women to follow him both emotionally and intellectually. That means being unafraid of the relationships that living entails and actively seeking to come to the light. It means learning from errors by being unafraid of admitting them and willing to seek correction: 'the man who lives by the truth, that is by the Spirit, comes into the light, so that it may be plainly seen that what he does is done in God' (3:21). The fear that would hold him back from so doing can be overcome by loving since loving is essentially an unobstructed acceptance of the other, whether material or personal, which enables what is potential to be realised. The call 'Follow me' made by Jesus is a call to 'be what you are', a child of God who is wholly concerned to bring you and his whole creation to its wholeness of living.

What hinders us then? Why do we not respond in this fearless fashion? There are few direct references in this gospel to the wellsprings of evil, though the words devil and Satan appear at critical points in the story. It is Jesus himself who replies to his critics by asking the questions just stated, in the words: 'Why can't you take in what I say?' (8:43). He answers it with the comment that they cannot do so because they fail to grasp his whole message about the true nature of life. Their failure is a matter of choice and not of inability. They prefer to act as the children of the devil, 'a murderer from the beginning' and 'the father of lies'. Once again we are faced with the demand to honour the Spirit of truth. The devil means literally 'the slanderer'. We slander those whom we fail to love. By permitting the slander to become a habit or tradition we build walls of hatred. Hence Jesus' critics retorted, 'Are we not right in saying you are a Samaritan and possessed by a devil?' (8:48). In his talk with the Samaritan woman Jesus had already shown that the wall being man-made could be thrown down by a person who refused to dishonour the Father by accepting it. He recognised the tension that existed and instead of taking refuge in an idealistic compromise accepted the challenge and acted upon it. A world which is plagued still by various types and degrees of apartheid has its most relevant sign-story in that event.

Yet another incident is used by John to carry further this thinking about the Spirit's work. To Jerusalem there had come at the time of the Passover certain Greeks, devout Gentiles, who having heard of Jesus were anxious to see him (12:21), though nothing further is said of anything approaching a mission to the Gentile world. John represents Jesus seeing in it the 'hour' in which through his death and resurrection his work is to be carried forward to embrace the whole world. It is the moment of glorification of the Son of Man. It represents therefore the overthrow of the devil who is the prince of this sundered world and the drawing of all men into the kingdom of God through him (12:31–32). It foretells the triumph of the Spirit of life.

But that end is not yet. The devil has one further stroke to make, suborning a chosen disciple to betray his Master (13:2). His is the choice of Death. Isolated from the environment of mutual love and trust brought into being by Jesus, Judas chooses to try to destroy it. The morsel of bread he received from Jesus we might say choked him. He would not remain any longer in that terrible tension of spirit 'but immediately went out into darkness'. There is no more apposite comment to be made than Othello's cry: 'the pity of it, Iago, the pity of it'. It was pity that moved Jesus to tell this stricken man to do what he had chosen to do as quickly as possible.

The scene in the upper room quite rightly becomes the occasion for the long-prepared moment of speaking fully about the gift of the Spirit. It directs the disciples' attention to the Advocate whom the Father will send in Jesus' name. His function is said to be that of teaching them and recalling what Jesus had said. It is a group that is being addressed, a prototype group of a new human society, a new tree of life symbolically spoken of as a vine. The transformation of the human social tradition not in Jewry only but in a much wider sphere is about to begin. The primary condition is that this body and its members should not be paralysed or deflected from proper growth by fear. The members must naturally support one another but do this in the power of the Advocate Spirit. They are not to be a self-confirming, self-justifying group whose unity is predetermined, but one that can receive and hold together the contraries that living introduces them to long and patiently enough to be able to resolve the tensions set up by moving on to new stages of relationship with one another. Their unity must be in the first place the psychic unity which was adumbrated in the experience of the children of Israel and which at some early stages in the history of other peoples was implanted in their members by acts of religious affirmation using symbols of death and rebirth.

But the spirit in John is not simply psyche but pneuma, a divinely given pneuma which John appears to have understood to mean that Spirit inbreathed into man, which moves him to be responsive to God. The band of disciples must learn to continue together after Jesus has gone from them. They will learn to do this by waiting upon and seeking guidance of the Holy Spirit. He will continue to demonstrate to them the things they had begun to see in their life with Jesus. He will carry them forward towards new stages of life. All this was promised to that small group of disciples who were to be the founding members of the church. The field of its action is nothing less than the whole world.

Now the gospel breaks off the story at the point where the Spirit is given, though written years later. The question that is inevitably raised in the mind of one reading it at any time afterwards is, how did they fare? What would someone reared in the Johannine tradition have wanted to say to the churches? Such questions are part of the praying which further reading of John's gospel will engender. It was to be expected that subsequent writing whether by the evangelist or someone close to him would be most anxious to discover the truth. What do the epistles and the Book of Revelation tell us of the further life of the Johannine churches?

Very clearly difficulties had arisen. One may trace in the First Epistle something very like a scrutiny of what has actually happened by someone who has re-read what the gospel had said about loving, about striving for unity, about confessing the Sonship of Jesus, and about overcoming the world. There is a strange bitterness in the word Antichrist referring to something very disruptive. There are a great many references to sins which have damaged the life of the church, to accusations, to refusals to love, to false prophets and lying. There is a bitter note in the statement that 'those rivals of Christ came out of our own number, but they had never really belonged; if they had belonged, they would have stayed with us; but they left us, to prove that not one of them ever belonged to us' (1 John 3:19). Whether the factions grew out of disputes about matters of doctrine or behaviour or administration we cannot know. In so demanding a venture of faith as the Christian communities took on every aspect of life could become as the evangelist had made clear in his gospel a temptation to fall back upon some mistaken promise of security. We can understand well enough what faults moved the writer of the Revelation to utter sharp warnings to the seven churches in Asia.

But praying the gospel requires more of us than noting these offences. What is asked of us as fellow Christians is simply more mature recognition of how such offences come and how in the strength of the indwelling spirit they may be forgiven. The centuries between our own day and that of the evangelist were to be prolific of the things which make up the history of Christendom:

> Time's handiworks by time are haunted,
> And nothing now can separate
> The corn and tares compactly grown.

The essential legacy of John however remains, as Edwin Muir described it:

> As clean as on the starting day[5]

and its truest manifestation is the outpouring of the Spirit of which the gospel-poem was one of its purest effusions and to which it was to recall hungry and eager souls from that time until now. The lives of the prophets, saints, artists, poets as much as those of the most ordinary men and women, are not success stories viewed in this dimension. They are compact of many defeats, wasted efforts, frequent disappointments and cruel failures, but their contribution has lain in the continuance of hope beyond all these things and is flowering in new gestures of trust in the Christ-Spirit alive with us still. 'They', as Jesus said in the prayer ascribed to him, 'are in the world' and 'in them I am glorified'.

Today in almost all continents there is evident an expression of fervent devotion centred upon the Spirit. It makes itself known in all denominations. Hans Küng in his book, *On Being a Christian*,[6] has summed up his reflections by saying: 'He allows himself to be inspired by the Spirit of the Scripture, who is in truth the Spirit of God and the Spirit of Jesus Christ'. He was to add further, in speaking of the Spirit, 'He is then, not a third party, not a thing between God and men, but God's personal closeness to men.' All of which may be true but still likely to raise much the same kind of problems as did that closeness of Jesus to the men of his generation. It is this that makes the Fourth Gospel the book most needed to be read and prayed in the world of today.

I said earlier that John somewhat strangely chose to leave

out many striking things that have belonged to the Christian story: no Lord's Prayer, no words recalling the eucharistic meal, no sending out men to baptise or to preach, no transfiguration, no Pentecostal public scene, no attempt to describe the Ascension. What he dwelt upon rather was that series of signs, the disturbances that they aroused, the conflict Jesus chose not to turn away from but to go through with the promise to those who trusted in him that the thing they had shared would not fail. In a special way that scene has returned to our world today. Lesslie Newbigin has put the question to us whether our modern world's culture is now in the throes of a more than normal self-questioning process or at a point of approaching its death. He himself has answered it in terms of the latter. His analysis in *The Other Side of 1984* will be unsatisfactory to many in its details. Never was mankind so possessed of power, so rich in achievements, so conscious of opportunities to remould the whole enterprise of human life as at this time. Yet Newbigin concludes: 'a brilliant culture is in danger of coming to an end. It has generated within itself destructive forces that it cannot hope in its present spiritual condition to control.'[7] Is this the point where the words 'I have overcome the world' no longer have meaning?

To those who might once have put that question to John he would have replied by asking them to read and pray his gospel, not simply the latter part of it but that troubled tempestuous narrative in which the world's problems and those of each man and woman were raised. Only by having eyes opened to what these problems really were could there be any satisfactory way forward revealed to mankind. Jesus is the revealer not simply of things concerning the nature of God which have then to be applied to life, but the revealer of the nature of things in which God is at work requiring mankind to find him there and give itself for the sake of the life of the children of God. John saw it in his day as a matter of stripping off many things that prevented men and women from doing that. They were there in political and religious institutions, in ancient behaviour patterns and modes of thought, in deep-seated personal fears and arid hostilities.

So it is likely to be today. The same need to set free the spirit in man to lay itself open to the pure Spirit of God is with us today. We must be ready to be exposed to that Spirit that Jesus spoke of when talking to Nicodemus. It can be greatly disturbing. At the second session of the Second Vatican Council a draft schema on the nature of the church was under discussion. One cardinal rose to protest that the document failed to mention the charisma or gifts of the Spirit that came often to lay Christians. It evoked a reply from another learned cardinal that though such things had happened in apostolic times, that age was now over. Since that time the Holy Spirit had spoken and speaks through the magisterium of the church. His objection was not sustained but it brought into the foreground many questions which press for consideration today. The anguish of a great many women who feel deeply that Christ's church has been well-nigh blinded to the true nature and calling of women, the pain that many priests and laypeople have endured when in their honest search for the truth they have met with indifference or condemnation from church officials. There is still the great heartache of the oppressed peoples of the world to be taken with greater seriousness than has yet been shown. We should do well to learn, for example, from Alice Walker's novel, *The Colour Purple*, what the letters of one sufferer addressed to Dear God have got to tell us. We have no less need to listen to a scholar like Geoffrey Lampe saying towards the end of his Bampton Lectures on 'God as Spirit' that he believed we needed that unifying concept more than the Trinitarian model for the articulation of our basic experience in the world today.

We take from the Fourth Gospel finally the great conviction that the Spirit of God is at work in the world, in the hearts of men and women, in young and old, in simple as well as talented people, in the failures and those apparently successful, in all faiths and nations. We take furthermore the demand of the Spirit that we be ready staff in hand and with expectation to move forward into a world as yet unknown. This also entails times of patient waiting, acceptance without

losing hope of manifest failures and grievous sins, times of
reconditioning to have new sense of initiative for the journey
ahead. It means finding the Spirit at work in all manner of
channels of events and human labour. It means learning as
Jesus of Nazareth did to listen, see, touch and taste all God-
given things that we may be the better equipped to respond
to this prompting Spirit. It also means being warned that the
Spirit blows where it listeth and, as Max Plowman wrote in
Bridge into the Future (1944), 'if you canalise the wind with a
stone drain-pipe it isn't the wind that you get but a draught'.
It means finally that we go on our way rejoicing in the day
that is still to come, the day when Jesus Christ's presence
through the Spirit is known to God's people on earth.

Appendix

The clergy of many churches have long been accustomed to the regular reading of the Psalter. The Psalms must in fact be among the most frequently recited poems in the world. They owe much of their influence to such use. In hoping that some men and women in all walks of life might be ready to use the Fourth Gospel in some such way, I venture to suggest a table of lections as a beginning.

I have kept in mind the fact that a great many people are not quite so free to order their timetable for such things as the clergy have been, so that the model of the monthly recitation of the Psalter, excellent as that has been, is not very practical here. Dividing it into portions for morning and evening use is likewise a little unrealistic. On the other hand some regular continued use is important. Reading it quietly but aloud and having time to reflect on each passage is also very desirable.

After much hesitation I decided to suggest that the gospel might be read four times during the year, each complete reading being spread over ninety days. Passages are bound to be unequal in length, as indeed are the Psalms. In the gospel one must take account of the narrative as well as the substance of the discourses ascribed to Jesus. My selection of such passages is simply for helping a reader. I can only claim that I have found it useful myself to follow the text in this way.

I would remind the reader that this is not asking for a

130

Bible study exercise in the commonly understood practice of such study. Let us by all means make good use of commentaries to enable us to understand the nature of the text of the gospel. This is perhaps better done at a time apart from the regular reading which I am advocating. In this latter our purpose is primarily that of praying. The reading is a way of learning to use John's poem, as my introduction suggests, as scaffolding to help the praying to become more workmanlike or a more deliberate engagement with what in the first instance prompted John to write his gospel.

This raises the question about what we understand by prayer. I would want to say as briefly as possible some things about it in the hope that this may help to clarify the purpose of such reading.

1   Prayer is the effort that each of us makes to be as honest as possible about life, our own, that of others we know, and of the society in which we live. This is what the Psalmist meant by asking for a clean heart. Prayer that does not strive to be honest is pseudo-prayer and not worth the time spent on it.

2   Because it is very difficult to be honest to God the old Jewish counsel about preparing to pray is of the utmost importance here. Some teachers said that the preparation was as important if not more so than the praying. It might give us pause to think what such honesty really means and what it asks of us in respect of our own personal life, our relations with others and with God. This goes a good deal deeper than the customary acts of self-examination and for that reason is best taken slowly. It has to be worked away at, which is why a regular effort is important.

3   It is important to remember that we are not alone in setting about this. Three times in John's gospel Jesus speaks of 'not being alone'. It is not our business to try to imagine ourselves in the presence of God but as simply as possible to remind ourselves that it is so.

4   We are also members of the whole family of God. The

gospel we are reading and trying to pray is about the life of that family, about its present condition and the hope of redemption. It is part of the business of being honest to remember this. In praying the gospel we are taking part in the history of the redemption of the world no less than those first disciples.

5 The Fourth Gospel is the great canticle of the Spirit at work in the world. It was written to sustain the hope of all those who look for the coming of God's kingdom on earth. We must learn to sing it, audibly or silently, by listening to it, by being anguished and delighted by it, as a documentary of the present-day world.

6 The Fourth Gospel did not promise the disciples a future free from tribulation, but one in which they would not be overcome. We are to read it as the lifeline that renews in us the sense of God coming into the world.

Appendix

A THREE-MONTHLY PLAN FOR READING THE FOURTH GOSPEL

1	1:1–5	31	7:31–38	61	14:1–12
2	1:6–9	32	7:39–53	62	14:13–21
3	1:10–13	33	8:1–11	63	14:22–26
4	1:14–18	34	8:12–19	64	14:27–31
5	1:19–32	35	8:20–30	65	15:1–6
6	1:33–39	36	8:31–38	66	15:7–17
7	1:40–51	37	8:39–45	67	15:18–27
8	2:1–12	38	8:46–59	68	16:1–12
9	2:12–30	39	9:1–17	69	16:13–19
10	2:13–25	40	9:18–34	70	16:20–28
11	3:1–15	41	9:35–41	71	16:29–33
12	3:16–21	42	10:1–10	72	17:1–11a
13	3:31–36	43	10:10–18	73	17:11b–19
14	4:1–14	44	10:19–33	74	17:20–23
15	4:15–25	45	10:34–42	75	17:24–26
16	4:26–42	46	11:1–16	76	18:1–14
17	4:43–54	47	11:17–27	77	18:15–27
18	6:1–15	48	11:28–44	78	18:28–40
19	6:16–27	49	11:45–57	79	19:1–13
20	6:28–40	50	12:1–8	80	19:14–22
21	6:41–51	51	12:9–19	81	19:23–30
22	6:52–58	52	12:20–24	82	19:31–37
23	6:59–71	53	12:25–28	83	19:38–42
24	5:1–18	54	12:29–36	84	20:1–10
25	5:19–30	55	12:37–43	85	20:11–18
26	5:31–38	56	12:44–46	86	20:19–23
27	5:39–47	57	12:47–50	87	20:24–31
28	7:1–12	58	13:1–20	88	21:1–14
29	7:13–24	59	13:21–32	89	21:15–19
30	7:25–30	60	13:33–38	90	21:20–25

References

Introduction

1 R. S. Thomas, 'Emerging', *Later Poems 1972–1982*. London, Macmillan, 1983. These lines, as published in *Laboratories of the Spirit* by R. S. Thomas, are quoted by permission of Macmillan, London and Basingstoke.

2 Dietrich Bonhoeffer, 'Letters to a Friend', *Letters and Papers from Prison*. London, Fontana, 1959.

3 W. Cantwell Smith, *The Meaning and End of Religion*. London, SPCK, 1978.

4 Johannes-Baptist Metz, *The Emergent Church*, London, SCM, 1981.

5 Bonhoeffer, op. cit.

6 Geza Vermes, *Jesus the Jew*. London, Collins, 1973.

7 D. Gascoyne, 'Ecce Homo', *Poems 1937–1942*. London, Poetry, 1943.

8 William Morris, *The Dream of John Ball* London, Longmans Green, 1924.

9 Iris Murdoch, *The Sovereignty of God*. London, Routledge & Kegan Paul, 1970.

10 W. Cantwell Smith, op. cit.

11 S. Sassoon, 'Testimony', *Selected Poems*. London, Faber, 1969.

1 The Book John Wrote

1 Henry Adams, *Mont St Michel and Chartres*. London, Constable, 1913.

2 W. H. Gombrich, *Symbolic Images*. London, Phaidon, 1975.

3 W. Shakespeare, *The Winter's Tale*.

4 M. K. Husayn, *City of Wrong*. Tr. K. Cragg, Amsterdam, 1939.

5 Simone Weil, *Waiting on God*. London, Collins, 1977.

6 Elie Wiesel, *Confronting the Holocaust*. Rosenfeld and Greenberg, Indiana University Press, 1978.

134

7 N. Micklem, *Behold the Man*. 1969.
8 B. Lindars, 'Commentary: The Gospel of John', New Century Bible. London, Marshall Morgan, 1972.

2 The Poem We Read

1 David Jones, *Epoch and Artist*. London, Faber, 1959.
2 Wallace Stevens, 'It must be abstract', *Selected Poems*. London, Faber, 1970.
3 R. P. Blackmur, *Language as Gesture*. London, Allen & Unwin, 1954.
4 T. S. Eliot, *Essays Ancient and Modern*. London, Faber, 1936.
5 Dame Helen Gardner, 'Religious Poetry'. Ewing Lectures 1966.
6 Thomas Hardy, 'The Self Unseeing', *Collected Poems*. London, Macmillan, 1928.
7 Frederick Franck, *The Zen of Seeing*. New York, Knopf, 1973.
8 Wallace Stevens, 'An Ordinary Evening in New Haven', *Selected Poems*. London, Faber, 1970.

3 Man

1 A. Heschel, *Who is Man?* London, Oxford University Press, 1966.
2 C. Sherrington, *Man on his Nature*. Cambridge University Press, 1963.
3 Sonnet XVII.
4 Heschel, op. cit.
5 Geza Vermes, op. cit.
6 C. Lévi-Strauss, *Tristes Tropiques*. London, Penguin, 1970.
7 L. L. Whyte, *The Next Development in Man*. London, Cresset Press, 1944.

4 Woman

1 Owen, *Acts of the Early Martyrs*. Oxford, Clarendon Press, 1927.
2 Karl Stern, *Flight from Woman*. London, Allen & Unwin, 1966.
3 D. Richardson, *Pointed Roofs*. London, Virago, 1982.
4 F. Rosenzweig, *The Star of Redemption*. London, Routledge & Kegan Paul, 1971.
5 Henry Adams, op. cit.
6 Stern, op. cit.

7 Mary Collins, qu. in *Concilium 182* (1955).
8 Israel Abrahams, *The Glory of God (Shekinah)*. Lectures, Oxford University Press, 1925.
9 S. T. Coleridge, *The Ancient Mariner*. 1800.
10 M. Rutherford, *Catherine Furze*. London, Hogarth Press, 1985.
11 E. Moltmann-Wendel, *The Women about Jesus*. London, SCM, 1982.
12 V. Watkins, 'Testimony', *The Death Bell*. London, Faber & Faber, 1954.
13 Meister Eckhart, in *Classics of Western Spirituality*. London, SPCK, 1982.
14 John Bayley, *The Characters of Love*. London, Chatto and Windus, 1961.
15 Browning, *A Death in the Desert*.
16 Ida Coudenhove, *The Nature of Sanctity*. London, Sheed & Ward, 1932.
17 Chinua Achebe, 'Refugee mother and child', in *Beware Soul Brother*. London, Heinemann, 1972.
18 Thomas Blackburn, 'Luna', *Selected Poems*. London, Hutchinson, 1975.

5 The Johannine Church

1 Laurens van der Post, *The Sword and the Doll*. London, Hogarth Press, 1963.
2 Raymond Brown, *The Community of the Beloved Disciple*. London, Chapman, 1979.
3 Raymond Brown, *The Churches the Apostles Left Behind*. London, Chapman, 1984.
4 W. H. C. Frend, *Saints and Sinners in the Early Church*. London, Darton, Longman & Todd, 1985.
5 Edwin Muir, 'The Journey Back', *Selected Poems*. London, Faber, 1965.

6 The Johannine Christ

1 Martin Buber, *Between Man and Man*. London, Kegan Paul, 1947.
2 Mary Douglas, *Natural Symbols*, London, Barrie & Rockliffe, 1970.
3 Norman Cohn, *The Pursuit of the Millennium*. London, Paladin, 1970.

4 H. Maccoby, *The Myth-Maker*, London, Weidenfeld & Nicolson, 1986.
5 Viktor Frankl, *The Doctor and the Soul*. London, Penguin, 1973.
6 Graham Sutherland, *Christ in Glory*. London, Zwemmer, 1964.
7 Chaim Potok, *My Name is Asher Lev*. London, Penguin, 1974.
8 James Dunn, *Christology in the Making*. London, SCM, 1980.
9 J. Pelikan, *Jesus Through the Centuries*. Yale University Press, 1985.
10 Potok, op. cit.

7   The Johannine Spirit

1 Browning, *A Death in the Desert*.
2 Geoffrey Lampe, *God as Spirit*. London, SCM, 1983.
3 Buber, op. cit.
4 Eckhart, op. cit.
5 Edwin Muir, 'One Foot in Eden', *Selected Poems*. London, Faber, 1965.
6 Hans Küng, *On Being a Christian*. London, Fount Paperbacks, 1978.
7 Lesslie Newbigin, *The Other Side of 1984*. London, World Council of Churches, 1983.